Jim Earl

Mourning Remembrance

Mourning Remembrance

Also by Jim Earl

How to Appease Your Stalker
Daddy, What's Sin-Eating?
Drinking to Win
Cure Loneliness and Cancer with Math
Learning the Internet with Porn
I Hate Everything About Myself and I Accept That
Great Stories I Never Wrote, and Other Things I Made Up
Mommy is Her Own Husband: A Hermaphrodite's Guide to Parenthood
Cooking for the Rapture: 'End of Times' Doesn't Have to Mean End of Eating

Jim Earl

Mourning Remembrance

A Collection of Mocking Obituaries Ripped from the Deadlines

By
Jim Earl

Illustrations by Nathan Smith
Cover art by Tony Millionaire

Mourning Remembrance

Copyright © 2006 by Jim Earl
Copyright © 2011 by Jim Earl
All rights reserved.
This book contains satire and other things.
ISBN 978-1467920384

Jim Earl

*When all the shithouse poets die
There will be erected in the sky
A monument of shit.*

Written on the men's room wall of Max's 540 Bar in San Francisco by "Anonymous," who is probably dead by now.

Mourning Remembrance

Jim Earl

CONTENTS

Acknowledgements 17

Foreword 19

Afterforeword 21

Art 23

Armand Fernandez Arman, French-American Sculptor 24

Joyce Ballantyne, Creator of the Coppertone Girl 26

Frank Gasparro, Lincoln Penny Designer 27

Flora Jacobs, World's Authority on Dollhouses 28

Pascal Kamar, Toymaker Who Created the Popular JFK and E.T. Dolls 29

Allen Kaprow, Expressionist Artist 30

Akira Yoshizawa, Origami Artist 31

Business 33

Joseph Barbera, Social Commentator 34

David Bushnell, Binocular King 35

Gerda Christian, Hitler's Personal Secretary 36

Herbert D. "Ted" Doan, Last of the Dows 37

Caleb Hammond Jr., Map Maker 38

Jim Heselden, Owner of The Segway Company 39

Betty James, Toy Maker Who Named The Slinky 42

Richard Kuklinski, Mafia Killer 44

Ken Lay, Math Expert 45

Slobodan Milosevic, Successful Banker 46

Helen Petrauskas, Top Safety Executive at Ford 48

Lawrence Rawl, Former Exxon Chairman 49

Nicolas M. Salgo, Famous Developer 50

Wilson A. Seibert Jr., Ad Man 51

Anna Nicole Smith, Estate Advisor 52

Chicago Crime Boss Albert Tocco 54

George Wackenhut, Security Expert 55

Charles Walgreen Jr., Drugstore King 56

John T. Walton, Heir to the Wal-Mart Fortune 58

Education 59

Frank Neuhauser, Winner Of The First National Spelling Bee 60

Exploration 63

William Irwin Wolff, M.D., Colonoscopy Pioneer 64

Jim Earl

Fashion..67

Don Fisher, Founder of The Gap..........................68

E.R. Haggar, Clothing Maker................................70

Food..71

Tobin Armstrong, Texas Cattle Rancher................72

Glen Bell, Founder of Taco Bell............................73

James Conway Sr., Founder of Mister Softee.......75

H. David Dalquist, Inventor of the Bundt Cake Pan...........77

Hilla Futterman, Expert on Preparing Meals From Weeds.79

Murray Handwerker, Owner of Nathan's Famous...............80

Harriet, the 176-Year-Old Giant Tortoise..............83

Dorothy Harmsen, Co-Founder of Jolly Rancher Candy Company..85

Margaret Karcher, Wife of the Founder of Carl's Jr............86

Bill Larson, Founder of Round Table Pizza.........87

Rose Mattus, Co-Founder of Haagen-Dazs........88

George Molchan, Oscar Mayer Mascot..............89

Nell Mondy, Potato Expert...................................91

Arnie Morton, Founder of Steakhouse Chain......92

Richard Nicholls, Father of the Gilroy Garlic Festival........93

Mourning Remembrance

W. Pauline Nicholson, Elvis Presley's Chef 94

Joseph L. Owades, Inventor of Light Beer 95

Frank Perdue, Chicken Choker 97

Mitchell Rupe, Convicted Killer Found Too Fat to Hang 99

Ruth Siems, Inventor of Stove Top Stuffing 100

Donald J. Tyson, Founder of Tyson Foods 102

Helen Ullrich, Nutritionist 104

Michael Vale, Star of 100 Dunkin' Donuts Commercials . 105

Heroism 107

Wesley Hill, Niagara Falls Rescuer 108

Invention 111

Samuel Alderson, Crash Test Dummy Inventor 112

George C. Ballas Sr., Inventor Of The Weed Eater 114

John Barron, Inventor of The ATM 115

Rebecca Carranza, Inventor of the Tortilla Chip 117

Samuel T. Cohen, Inventor of The Neutron Bomb 119

Harry Wesley Coover Jr., Inventor of Super Glue 121

Bertram Given, Inventor of the Garbage Disposal 123

Ronald Howes, Inventor of the Easy-Bake Oven 124

Jim Earl

Robert Kearns, Inventor of Intermittent Wipers 125

Richard LaMotta, Creator of the Chipwich Ice Cream Sandwich 127

Milton Levine, Inventor of The Ant Farm 128

Philip Morrison, A-Bomb Inventor 130

Elwood Perry, Maker of a Fishing Lure 131

Robert Rich, Inventor of Nondairy Whipped Topping 133

Gerry Thomas, Inventor of the TV Dinner 134

Arch West, Creator of Doritos 136

Morrie Yohai, Inventor of the Cheez Doodle 137

Mike Yurosek, Inventor of 'Baby' Carrots 139

Literary **141**

Shelby Foote, Civil War Historian and Novelist 142

Dale Messick, Creator of 'Brenda Starr' Reporter 144

Lyle Stuart, Controversial Book Publisher 145

Max Velthuijs, Author of Popular Children's Books 146

Medicine **149**

Daniel Ruge, President Reagan's White House Physician .. 150

Jack Scholl, Foot-Care Pioneer 152

Charles Socarides, the Psychiatrist Who Said Gays Could Become Straight. 153

William G. Speed, Migraine Expert 154

Leo Sternbach, Creator of Valium 155

Military 157

Edward N. Hall, Father of the Minuteman Missile 158

Samuel Koster, General Charged in My Lai Massacre 160

Bruce Peterson, the Real "Six Million Dollar Man" 161

Albert L. Weimorts, Designer of Big Bombs 163

General William Westmoreland, Vietnam War General ... 164

Music 167

James Griffin, Co-Founder of the Band Bread 168

Eric Griffiths, Guitarist for the Quarrymen. 170

Eugene Landy, Brian Wilson's 24-Hour A Day Therapist. 171

Robert Moog, Creator of the Moog Synthesizer 172

Lucy Vodden, Music Victim 173

Pioneers 175

John Diebold, Computer Visionary 176

Maurice Graham, King of the Hobos 177

Jim Earl

Chet Helms, Father of San Francisco's Summer of Love .. 179

Steve Jobs, "Dear Leader" 180

Paul K. Keene, Organic Farming Pioneer 182

Jef Raskin, Macintosh Computer Pioneer 183

Paul Sawyer, NASCAR Pioneer 184

Ed Schantz, Botox Pioneer 185

Politics **187**

General Sani Abacha, Nigerian Dictator 188

Lou Carrol, the Man Who Gave Nixon the Dog Checkers 189

Michael Evans, Ronald Reagan's Photographer 190

Michael S. Joyce, Conservative 191

Edward von Kloberg III, PR Man to the Dictators 192

Helen Murphy, White House Gift Shop Manager 193

Paul K. Perry, Political Statistician 194

J.B. Stoner, White Supremacist 195

Caspar Weinberger, Reagan's Secretary of Defense 196

Religion **199**

Owen Allred, Polygamous Leader 200

Susan Atkins, Born Again Christian 201

Mourning Remembrance

Rosemary Kooiman, Pagan Witch 203

Osama bin-Laden, Billionaire Industrialist, Businessman, Entrepreneur, Religious Icon & Chick Magnet 204

Anton LaVey, Spiritual Leader 207

Henry Morris, Father of Modern Creationism..................209

Adrian P. Rogers, Tool of God..210

Science 211

Alastair Cameron, Developed Giant Impact Theory 212

Sidney Gottlieb, LSD Scientist..213

Horace Hagedorn, Fertilizer Giant 215

George Lenchner, Prominent Mathematician...................217

John DeLorean, Famed Chemist.......................................218

Jacob Marinsky, Discovered Promethium 220

Maynard J. Ramsay, Renowned Buggerer........................221

Show Business 223

Lew Anderson, Clarabell the Clown on Howdy Doody 224

Henry Corden, Voice of Fred Flintstone...........................226

Gerard Damiano, Director of the Film Deep Throat 227

Bob Denver, Actor. Roll Model. Gilligan. 229

Lillian Bounds Disney, Wife of Walt 231

Jim Earl

James Dougherty, Marilyn Monroe's First Husband..........232

Len Dresslar, Voice of The Jolly Green Giant 233

Ralph Edwards, TV Pioneer 234

George Gerbner, Television Researcher 236

Phil Harris, Captain on Deadliest Catch, and Advocate of the Inverted Food Pyramid 237

Paul Henning, Television Producer 240

Bob Kane, Not Bob Crane 242

Gordon Lee, Child Star in the Little Rascals 244

Sid Luft, Judy Garland's Third Husband 245

Vaughn Meader, JFK Mimic 246

Ted Peshak, Director of Educational-Films 247

Thurl Ravenscroft, the Voice of Tony the Tiger 248

Celebrity Dwarf, John Rice 249

Nipsey Russell, Comedian 251

Theodore F. Shaker, Former CEO of Arbitron Ratings Company 252

Spoony Singh, Founder of Hollywood Wax Museum 253

Peter Smithers, Model for James Bond 255

Aaron Spelling, Artist 256

Herbert L. Strock, B-Movie Director 258

Lennie Weinrib, Voice of H.R. Pufnstuf 259

Thelma White, Actress 260

Robert Young, Actor...261

Sports 263

Arnold Denker, 'Dean of American Chess'......................264

Ben Hogan, Golf Legend..265

Annotation of Jim Earl's Mourning Remembrance 267

Afterword..271

Jim Earl

Acknowledgements

Thanks to Tony Millionaire for the art on the outside of the book.

Thanks to Nathan Smith for the art on the inside of the book.

And thanks to everyone for eventually dying. Great job!

Mourning Remembrance

Jim Earl

Foreword

Jim Earl is a pain in the ass but he is a pain in the ass with a purpose and that's what sets him apart from other pains in the ass. He has principles and values and he had the courage to let those things cripple his career and make him a bitter, cantankerous old man. Fortunately those character traits have had absolutely no negative impact on his comedy genius. Quite the contrary. Jim has a vision unlike anyone else. It is pure, original, hilarious, and mostly wrong. There is nothing funnier than wrong when it is done right. Jim does it right.

I first met Jim in San Francisco when he was part of the comedy team Lank and Earl. Maybe there is some footage of them out there you can look at. I don't know. Hang on. Wait, there is. Hahaha, they were funny. Jim was the cute dark doofus to Barry Lank's aggravated Jewish straight guy. Wow, they were good. Wonder what went wrong with that act. Not my business. Ask Jim. I'm sure it's a long story and he was the victim somehow. God, I love this guy.

Jim also wrote for the Daily Show and if you ask him about that he will talk about it endlessly. He will give you an entirely new perspective on what has come to be known as one of the best comedy shows in the history of history. After talking to Jim for as long you can take, you will walk away thinking, "I had no idea Jon Stewart was the dictator of a Third World Country." Man, Jim Earl and his famous Daily Show stories have cleared tables full of funny people eating and trying to have a good time with their peers coast to coast.

Well, wait, that's unfair of me. The reason you don't want to eat with Jim is because he is a Vegan, an angry Vegan. You shouldn't eat with Jim unless you want the excitement of eating a burger diminished by an Earlian dissertation on the horrors of cow farts and their effects on the ozone and agriculture. Maybe just have an appetizer or some fries. He's cool with spuds. I think he is. Jeez, you better check with him.
I don't want to come off as being anti Jim because this is for his book and we are here to celebrate him like he is dead and left us this pile of writings. I worked with Jim on two radio shows. He created and wrote original comedy bits like nothing I have ever heard and he did it consistently. Many of the pieces in this book were born out of those bits. He is a genius. I don't use that word lightly. I use it here with medium intensity. I mean, this isn't science we're talking about, it's comedy. Jim's ability to satirically level religion, stupidity, death, media, celebrity and ignorance is unparalleled. He does it poetically and with a true uniqueness.

To be honest, Jim Earl is a sweet soft spoken man with a big heart, but just beneath his moral fortitude and seeming tranquility is a raging river of bile and darkness. These pages are filled from the buckets from that well.

Just so you know, I'm sure if you ask Jim about me and pressed him a bit he would have some pretty shitty things to say. You know what? I wish you would and get back to me. Thanks.

Enjoy Jim's things.

Marc Maron

Jim Earl

Afterforeword

From the beginning of time, humans have been dying at the rate of about one person per death. I think we can do better than that.

What do we really know about death? Science tells us that death is preferable to an Adam Sandler movie. To the dying, death means making peace with the past before saying farewell to loved ones. To the bereaved, it means fighting over who gets that collection of glass insulators in the kitchen.

We mustn't forget that shortly before he took the oath of office as President of the United States, Batman described America as, "A loose confederation of prisons, coal mines and gun factories, copiously dotted with memorials and cemeteries." And who can argue with that?

All I'm saying is, if you think you're dead, then you're probably alive. However, if you think you're alive, then you probably should be dead, because most likely you're annoying everyone around you.

Lastly, I can't believe you paid good money for this.

Well, that about sums it up. I dedicate this book to the American housing industry, which is dead.

Jim Earl

Mourning Remembrance

Jim Earl

Art

Mourning Remembrance

Armand Fernandez Arman, French-American Sculptor

Armand Fernandez Arman, the nouveau-realist artist who achieved fame by assembling sculptures out of everyday objects, died recently after soldering his pacemaker to a cheese grater and calling it, "Help, I Just Soldered My Pacemaker to a Cheese Grater."

Arman first got the idea to start making art out of burned and mangled objects after seeing someone react to his art by burning and mangling it.

In one 1959 exhibit, the controversial artist filled a Paris gallery with rubbish, causing a scandal, while at the same time creating the world's largest repository of Jerry Lewis films.

Jim Earl

His use of discarded objects and old junk was the inspiration for many great artists. And the comedy of Carrot Top.

At one point, he reportedly had more recycled garbage than NBC's fall lineup.

Friends say Arman devoted the last years of his life to trying to dig himself out of the world's biggest pile of crap.

Arman requested his remains be cut apart, cremated, and then cleverly reattached atop a pedestal with a broken violin.

Joyce Ballantyne, Creator of the Coppertone Girl

Eighty-eight, year-old Joyce Ballantyne, the artist responsible for the iconic American image of the bare-bottomed Coppertone Girl, died of embarrassment last week when a mischievous basset hound pulled down her adult diaper at a local bingo game.

Within months after its release in 1955, Ballantyne's image of the little girl and the dog became synonymous with Coppertone, and later, skin cancer.

Throughout the years, Ballantyne's image carried such slogans as "Don't Be a Paleface," followed by "Tan, Don't Burn," and the more recent, "Okay. This Isn't What You Think It Is. You're Under Arrest."

For two decades, Ballantyne was also an illustrator for *Sports Afield* magazine, creating the iconic image of a bear pulling off the bottom of a hunter's leg.

Ballantyne is survived by millions of baby boomers with the hideous skin of an old, wrinkled purse.

Jim Earl

Frank Gasparro, Lincoln Penny Designer

Frank Gasparro, former chief engraver at the U.S. Mint and designer of the tail side of the Lincoln Penny, is permanently out of circulation.

The 92-year-old apparently drowned after a young couple threw him into a wishing well.

News of his death came as a shock to loved ones, who had believed he was in good, but worn condition.

Gasparro was appointed chief engraver at the U.S. Mint by President Lyndon Johnson in 1965 but had to leave under a storm of protest after the debut of his unpopular "My Lai Massacre Nickel."

Family members recall that whenever people unfamiliar with his work asked where they might find some examples, he would reply, "It's in your pocket," leading to the widespread misconception that Gasparro invented the lint-covered condom.

It was Gasparro's last wish that his remains be flattened by a locomotive.

Flora Jacobs, World's Authority on Dollhouses

Flora Jacobs, the internationally recognized authority on dollhouses and miniature furniture, died last month when a giant cat jammed its paw through her bedroom window and chewed on her for ten minutes before losing interest and walking off.

Jacobs founded the now famous Washington Dolls' House and Toy Museum back in 1975, starting with nothing more than a big dream and a tiny library of law books abandoned by the Nixon administration.

At its peak, the museum attracted more than 20,000 visitors a year, most of them concerned psychiatrists.

Jacobs had to close the museum in 2004 after Michael Jackson kept sleeping with residents of her miniature Ronald McDonald House.

Jacobs requested her body be placed inside a real-sized coffin. Seriously. Enough is enough already.

Jim Earl

Pascal Kamar, Toymaker Who Created the Popular JFK and E.T. Dolls

Pascal Kamar, who in early 1963 became a millionaire with the debut of his 11-inch President Kennedy doll, is dead after 30 disappointing years of trying to unload a warehouse full of Martha Moxley hand puppets.

At first Kamar couldn't make enough JFK dolls to keep up with demand. But when that fateful day arrived on November 22, 1963, sales went down faster than Marilyn Monroe on Peter Lawford's yacht.

In 1982 he signed a licensing agreement to produce the E.T. doll. The move not only saved his business, it also enabled countless American children to realize their dream of cuddling up against something that looks like a mummified fetus.

Always the marketing genius, Kamar was able to meet the demands of delivering millions of the wrinkled, potbellied creatures on time by making only slight modifications to his surplus of LBJ dolls.

Kamar requested his body be hollowed out, stuffed with beans, cotton and straw, and sold to a guy who gets off dressing like a hedgehog.

Allen Kaprow, Expressionist Artist

Allen Kaprow, the 1960s artist who broke new ground in expression by staging events he called "happenings," is now expressing himself by "not happening."

Kaprow's body was found sprawled on a canvas stained with two overturned cans of acrylic paint and paw prints from his basset hound, Grover. Friends called it "his greatest work."

One of Kaprow's best-known pieces was "Yard," consisting of a jumble of spare tires heaped in a small room open to foot traffic. This was quickly followed by "What the Hell is My Son Doing with His Life?" consisting of his mother standing in a small room open to foot traffic pleading, "What the hell is my son doing with his life?"

The deceased requested his remains be left in a phone booth with a paper bag and a turnip.

Jim Earl

Akira Yoshizawa, Origami Artist

Akira Yoshizawa, the Japanese origami master whose expressive paper creations made an art out of his country's tradition of shame and repressed emotions, died of heart failure after frustrated doctors were unable to unfold his "please resuscitate" orders in time.

Legend has it that Akira's first encounter with origami came at the age of 3 when a neighbor folded him a boat and told him to attack Pearl Harbor.

Akira became an expert in origami during World War II when in order to teach geometry to younger colleagues at the factory where he worked, he folded paper models. A practice the Japanese Army later adopted to help bridge the language barrier between soldiers and Korean sex-slaves.

Yoshizawa requested his remains be folded carefully with the right top fold placed on top of the center fold of the diamond. Repeat steps 9 through 12. To inflate, blow into small hole at bottom as indicated by arrow. You now have a frog.

Mourning Remembrance

Jim Earl

Business

Joseph Barbera, Social Commentator

Joseph Barbera, who teamed with William Hanna to torture generations of American children with the worst animation in cartoon history, died of injuries last week after the confused 95 year-old tried to dress a 500-pound brown bear in a porkpie hat and starched collar.

Stunned paramedics who arrived at the scene declared him "Deader than the average cartoonist."

Barbera is best loved for creating animated domestic sitcoms like *The Jetsons*, *The Flintstones*, and a spin-off based on the Flintstones' quirky neighbors, *The Manstone Family*. In one famous episode, after the character Sharon Slatestone is murdered, a baby wooly mammoth being used to vacuum up the crime scene turns to the camera and mugs, "It's a living."

When reached for comment, Scooby Doo said quote, "Rell, ree ras rallways a real rig rinfluence ron re. Ry reremember rone rime rwen Rister Rarrera rasked ree rye I ricked ry ralls. And rye ranswered, 'Rerause I can.' Ra ra ra ra. Ruh rooh. Scooby sad."

Mourners include OJ Simpstone, Boutros Boutros Ghallstone, John Kenneth Gallstone's son, James Kenneth Gallstone, Bill Clintstone, Michael Jackstone, Stone Phillipstone, and a guy named John Smith.

The deceased requested his remains be buried accompanied by hilarious "skidaddle" sound effects.

Jim Earl

David Bushnell, Binocular King

David Bushnell, founder of Bushnell Binoculars, died last week after a long period of shifting in and out of focus.

Bushnell started the business back in 1948 when he imported his first two crates of binoculars to the states and helped introduce millions of middle-class Americans to the bathroom windows of millions of other middle-class Americans.

Ironically, the company is now based in Kansas, a place where there's absolutely nothing to look at.

Bushnell requested his body be polished, kept out of the sun, and put back in its case, damn it. Or they'll be hell to pay this time. You damn kids have no respect for my possessions. This time it's coming out of your allowance. Do you want the belt?

Mourning Remembrance

Gerda Christian, Hitler's Personal Secretary

Gerda Christian, Adolf Hitler's personal secretary and witness to his suicide in a Berlin bunker, died at the age of "dreiundachzig" after her heart "Gestapoed."

As Hitler's secretary in the bunker, her duties were "filing, typing, and always making sure there was fresh cyanide in the water cooler."

According to Gerda, Hitler was obsessed with tender memories of his youth, playing sports, flirting with girls, and lying on his back underneath glass coffee tables.

She recalled how the pudgy bunker crackup, Hermann Goering, never failed to get a hearty guffaw from Adolf whenever he donned his "Battle of the Bulge" tee-shirt.

But all good things come to an end. And within two days after marrying Eva Braun, Hitler killed himself, explaining in a note, "I just couldn't take the head games anymore. She was too controlling."

Gerda feared her years as Hitler's secretary might keep her from gainful employment because in order to fill out the section labeled "Reason for leaving previous job" on a job application, she'd have to answer, "World not ready for master race."

Gerda leaves behind a few relatives still in hiding and favored mementos from her secretarial years including her, "It must be Montag" coffee mug, and a comical poster with the phrase, "You don't have to be Aryan to work here, but it helps."

Jim Earl

Herbert D. "Ted" Doan, Last of the Dows

Herbert "Ted" Doan, the last family member to lead Dow Chemical, the world's largest producer of plastics, chemicals and synthetic rubber, is now breaking down into smaller and smaller pieces. But ultimately he will never disappear.

Doan apparently died of asphyxiation after the Dow Silly Putty he was pleasuring himself with became hopelessly stuck in the tracks of the Dow Ziploc bag he was erotically tightening around his head.

Soon after becoming head of Dow Chemical, Doan vowed to increase growth by ten percent per year. Unfortunately he was talking about tumors.

Founded by his grandfather in 1897 on the principal that there weren't enough three-eyed fish in the world, Dow today leaks even more dioxin than those old batteries in Mary Cheney's vibrator.

Over the years the world's largest producer of fake breasts gave millions of dollars to the Saginaw Valley State University, culminating with the erection of the Doan Science Building – made completely out of defective "double-D's."

Doan requested his body be used to coat Rosie O'Donnell's new waffle iron.

Caleb Hammond Jr., Map Maker

Caleb D. Hammond, former president of C. S. Hammond & Company, map makers, is dead after a piece of plaque took a wrong turn down a pulmonary artery and crashed into his aorta.

Mr. Hammond's grandfather, Caleb, started the company over a century ago with nothing more than an "x" and the word "treasure" tattooed on a dead sailor's chest.

Hammond was second only to Rand McNally in producing atlases pinpointing cities, towns, and countries all around the world that George W. Bush could never identify.

At any one time more than 100 cartographers might be working for the company, each one ignoring his wife's desperate pleas to look at the map before driving any further.

In 1999, the company was sold to Langenscheidt Publishers, a German company that originally made its fortune selling South American travel guides to members of the SS.

Hammond requested his body be folded up like an accordion and crammed into the glove compartment of his family's station wagon.

Jim Earl

Jim Heselden, Owner of The Segway Company

Jim Heselden, owner of the Segway Company, is no longer owner of the Segway Company. Little did he know when he bought the company last December, that he'd be buying the farm this month.

Witnesses say Heselden was riding one of his scooters when it apparently scooted him over a 50-foot cliff into a river of scooter death.

Police found his body near the wrecked machine where paramedics pronounced him "hilarious."

According to the investigation, officials said his multiple injuries were consistent with that of an idiot's.

Mourning Remembrance

A generous man, Heselden is credited with donating over 1,000 Segways to disabled veterans, who are now trying to donate them to the Taliban.

In case you've never driven one, you lean forward to go forward, lean back to go backward, and lean left to lurch suddenly down a 50-foot cliff into a ravine.

The scooter was the subject of a massive recall in 2006 due to a software glitch that could cause the unit to kill millionaires.

And back in 2003, Segway's image took a hit when George W. Bush fell off one while negotiating an unusually difficult crevasse in Barbara Bush's cave-like womb.

His death highlights five safety precautions riders should take when using a Segway:

Number One:
Don't buy one.

Number Two:
If you do buy one, don't buy one.

Number Three:
Okay, so you bought one. Now put it in storage.

Number Four:
Always wear brightly colored clothing so police can easily find your mangled body at the bottom of a ravine.

Number Five:
If you wake up in the middle of the night to find one hovering over your bed, do not make eye contact. Remember, as Judy Garland well documented in her experiences filming The Wizard of Oz, the little Segways are incorrigible pranksters

Jim Earl

who have insatiable sexual appetites. Try to distract their attention with cigars and alcohol. Then back away slowly while they pass out with their erections in their hands.

Family members are consoling themselves with the thought that right now Heselden's up in Heaven, jammin' with somebody who also got killed by a funny invention. Yeah, I didn't do a lot of research on that last joke.

Heselden requested his body be strapped to a Segway and stuck in a cornfield to scare away crows.

Betty James, Toy Maker Who Named The Slinky

Betty James, the woman responsible for naming the Slinky, is dead after tumbling down a flight of stairs into a heating grate.

Apparently her momentum caused her body to bounce end-over-end from one step to the next, much to the delight of a girl and a boy.

Her husband, a ship engineer, conceived of the toy in 1943 after watching an IUD pop out of Tallulah Bankhead while she was dedicating a minelayer.

Seventeen years later, the inventor abandoned the family to join a religious cult dedicated to worshiping those little springs you find in push-button pens.

Jim Earl

Though the Slinky was developed to be a toy, U.S. soldiers in Vietnam liked to use it as an antenna. Similarly, the Viet Cong liked to use the commercial jingle to torture John McCain.

During her lifetime, hundreds of millions of plastic Slinkys were sold to children around the world. You can now find them in the Gulf of Mexico wrapped around the necks of millions of pelicans.

James requested one end of her elongated body be twisted and then suddenly released in order to demonstrate transverse wave motion.

Richard Kuklinski, Mafia Killer

Richard Kuklinski, who claimed to have killed more than 100 people as a Mafia hit man, died of shame this month when it was revealed he only killed 99.

Kuklinski often listed the many ways he killed, including guns, ice picks, hand grenades, chainsaws and crossbows. But experts agree his most effective weapon was "eerie shunning."

After committing his first murder at 14, Kuklinski said he felt, "empowered," a word Oprah would later use to murder daytime television.

Kuklinski later became known as the Iceman because he would often freeze corpses to disguise the time of death and then sell them as props to Martin Scorsese.

The deceased requested his remains be stuffed into the trunk of a late model domestic sedan and be mistaken for Jimmy Hoffa.

Jim Earl

Ken Lay, Math Expert

Ken Lay, the man who founded Enron Corporation and cheated thousands of employees out of their pensions, topped himself last night by cheating thousands of hungry prisoners out of their chance to make him their cell bitch.

Lay apparently died of a massive coronary at his vacation home after unsuccessfully trying to funnel somebody else's life savings up his pulmonary artery.

Lay's servants were reportedly so upset when they found the body, they barely had time to light a couple of roman candles between his legs before the paramedics arrived.

George Bush's largest contributor, Lay was originally chosen to be the President's Secretary of Treasury in 2000, but turned it down when it was argued he could commit more crimes in the private sector.

Family members are consoling themselves with the thought that Lay is now driving the 7th level of Hell into bankruptcy.

Mourning Remembrance

Slobodan Milosevic, Successful Banker

Former Yugoslav president Slobodan Milosevic died last week of a prescription drug reaction in his prison cell, apparently after finding David Crosby's old stash.

A ruthless advocate of bloodthirsty nationalism, Milosevic unleashed ten years of "ethnic cleansing" that recast the map of Europe and helped inspire the most successful parts of the Wolfowitz doctrine.

As a youth, Milosevic was a pudgy loner with no friends. But as the years passed, he gradually matured into an old pudgy loner with no friends.

In 1962 while Milosevic was in college, his domineering father committed suicide by shooting himself, and his mother hanged herself 11 years later. It was probably the worst reaction to bad mid-semester grades ever.

Milosevic requested his remains be divided amongst his family in Moscow and his scrotum be put back in the Balkans.

Joke Diagram: "Scrotum" - put back in the - Bal kans or "ball cans." This joke alone is worth more than the price of this book. Stop complaining.

Helen Petrauskas, Top Safety Executive at Ford

Helen Petrauskas, a controversial safety executive at Ford motors, reportedly died of frustration last week when the fuel tank on the Ford ambulance she was in caught fire minutes after the tire on the Explorer she'd been driving blew out while her car was suddenly leaping from park to reverse and stalling on a left turn and then exploding.

More than anyone, Petrauskas was responsible for putting air bags in cars in 1990, tragically 20 years after they could have prevented the injury that inspired VH1's *Leif Garret: Behind the Music*.

Petrauskas was born 61 years ago in Ukraine, where today things are so bad, air bags are often sold into prostitution.

She was three days old when her family fled the country in a horse-drawn wagon, the safest vehicle she'd ever ride in.

The deceased requested her body be exploded at 200 miles per hour into the face of a drunk teenage driver with braces.

Jim Earl

Lawrence Rawl, Former Exxon Chairman

Lawrence Rawl, chairman and CEO of Exxon Corporation during the Valdez oil disaster in Alaska, died last week at his Fort Worth home, reportedly after his bursting bladder befouled some 6,000 square feet of executive real estate and killed scores of watery-eyed poodles.

Under his leadership, Rawl reduced costs at Exxon by selling subsidiaries, closing service stations, and giving tanker captains longer unpaid cocktail breaks.

Rawl was also responsible for moving Exxon's headquarters from New York to Texas, basically because people expect less there.

Environmental experts estimate that even with the use of high-pressure steam hoses, detergent and sawdust, it may take years to completely remove Rawl's remains from the living room carpet.

Mourning Remembrance

Nicolas M. Salgo, Famous Developer

Nicolas M. Salgo, conservative Republican financier and builder of the infamous Watergate Hotel complex in Washington D.C., has finally checked out.

According to doctors, Salgo was declared dead after reportedly suffering an "18 minute gap in brain activity."

Salgo was the principal developer behind the Watergate Hotel and ingeniously attracted patrons by offering a special discount for any guests willing to, quote, "Have their dainties fondled by G. Gordon Liddy."

Over the years, Salgo took on many differing projects, including a ranching operation in Oregon noted for employing the only cowhands ever to have had their phones tapped in the name of national security.

Memorial services will be held before noon to avoid being charged for an extra day.

Jim Earl

Wilson A. Seibert Jr., Ad Man

Wilson A. Seibert, the man responsible for some of Madison Avenue's most memorable advertising campaigns, is now taking a much anticipated commercial break from life.

During his career, Mr. Seibert won numerous honors for his unparalleled humanitarian work helping orphans and victims of AIDS. Ha. Just kidding, he only won them for writing ads.

One poster of an ad he did for the Marines with the slogan, "We don't promise you a rose garden," was placed on display at the Smithsonian Institution right next to his subsequent slogan,
"We also don't promise you an education, pension, medical care or your life back either, so shut up and fight, you insect. You're parents think you're dead and the president's forgotten you. Oh, and don't even *think* of kissing another man on the lips, even if you *can* speak Arabic."

Seibert also wrote the famous cigarette jingle that went, "Chesterfield 101's: A silly millimeter longer," a phrase describing the cigarette's length as well as the daily growth rate of the average lung tumor.

Seibert requested his burial be preceded by an announcement that completely misrepresents his body's actual ingredients.

Mourning Remembrance

Anna Nicole Smith, Estate Advisor

Anna Nicole Smith, former Playboy centerfold, actress and retirement complex for 90-year-old penises, died last week at the Seminole Hard Rock Cafe Hotel and Casino in Hollywood, Florida. What a surprise!

Cause of death was not immediately known, but authorities speculate Smith may have stopped breathing after tripping headfirst into her portable mayonnaise fountain.

Paramedics said when they rolled Smith over, they found two day-laborers tragically smothered after trying to enter the country illegally beneath her breast flaps.

After repeatedly failing to restore her heartbeat, doctors declared Smith brain dead at 2:49 p.m., 1983.

Jim Earl

The famous blonde was just thirty-nine – hundred pounds.

In the hours before she died, friends say Smith appeared incoherent and wasted. In other words, completely normal.

Police say Smith's hotel suite was filled with prescription drugs, all of them administered with Crisco.

The drugs included Xanax, Vicodin, Methadone, and a combination of the three she liked to call, "Xanaxo-Dinadone."

When he learned of the death, Zsa Zsa Gabor's husband revealed he might be the father of Smith's daughter. He also hinted DNA tests might be in order for Mister Haney and Arnold the Pig. Yeah I know it's the wrong Gabor sister. Get off my back.

Smith requested her remains be buried next to a very rich corpse.

Mourning Remembrance

Chicago Crime Boss Albert Tocco

Chicago crime boss Albert Tocco died of a stroke this month, after a chunk of fat put out a contract on his left aorta.

Tocco controlled the Chicago suburbs, mainly by extorting protection money from Humvee owners to defend against their liberal neighbors' withering remarks about gas mileage.

In 1986 his wife testified that Tocco admitted killing Las Vegas crime boss Tony "the Ant" Spilotro. The Spilotro case was the basis for the film, *Casino*, another crime Tocco should have been charged with.

Mr. Tocco, whose nickname was Caesar, went to prison 15 years ago for racketeering, conspiracy, and being part of an amusing cultural anomaly where people have names like "Caesar" and "Ant."

Mrs. Tocco, who is believed to be the first mob wife to ever testify against her husband, is now living safely in the federal witness protection program at 201 14th Street in Seattle – whoops.

Tocco's victims requested his remains be crammed into the trunk of a 1972 Chevy Impala while a tape loop plays "Shaddup You Face."

Jim Earl

George Wackenhut, Security Expert

George R. Wackenhut, former F.B.I. agent, disciplinarian and owner of the Wackenhut Corporation, an international security firm that promotes the use of private guards at prisons, died of a heart attack after mumbling something about, "spending a night in the box just to see what it's really like."

To impress potential clients, Mr. Wackenhut liked to dress his guards up in helmets and paratrooper boots. It wasn't until years later that he decided to add pants.

Still a growing concern, the Wackenhut Corporation has been accused of abusing inmates in Florida, Texas and Louisiana, and soon hopes to expand to beating and starving prisoners in the Midwest and Northern states as well.

At the time of his death, Wackenhut controlled more than 40,000 prison beds around the world, making his company the largest sponsor of sodomy outside Neverland ranch.

Mourning Remembrance

Charles Walgreen Jr., Drugstore King

Charles Walgreen Jr., who helped build his father's business into this country's most reliable source for drugs since the CIA, died last week after he failed to open the childproof lid on a little thing called "life."

Born in Chicago 100 years ago, Walgreen watched his father start the family business using nothing more than a little gumption* and half a bottle of ipecac.

Trained as a pharmacist, Walgreen served as the company's president from 1939 until 1963, when he was hired as Elvis Presley's personal cook.

Jim Earl

In the 1950s Walgreen revolutionized the retail drug business by making it self-service. Before that, abortion hangers were only available from *behind* the counter.

In retirement, he obtained an ocean captain's license and sailed around the world on a yacht powered on nothing but Wal-Tussin.

And at the age of 95, Walgreen sailed to the Galapagos Islands where he became the first person in history to make an iguana wait in line 30 minutes for the wrong medication.

Walgreen requested his remains be located conveniently throughout America so that every neighborhood can have access to affordable old-man parts.

* *See obituaries for Murray Handwerker and Don Fisher for more about gumption and its various uses.*

Mourning Remembrance

John T. Walton, Heir to the Wal-Mart Fortune

Wal-Mart board member John T. Walton rolled back prices for the last time this week after rolling his airplane at high speed into the Grand Teton National Park.

According to a company spokesman, the Wal-Mart executive was apparently scouting endangered grizzly bear populations for cheap, non-union labor.

Last March, Walton was listed by Forbes Magazine as the world's 11th richest person in addition to being one of only three people in the world who would build an ugly, life-sucking superstore within eye-view of a sacred, pre-Columbian pyramid.

Walton died in an experimental, ultra light aircraft wrapped in a fabric similar to the heavy-duty tents many Wal-Mart employees have to live in outside the store.

In loving tribute to Walton's memory, Wal-Mart's worldwide employees were issued an extra cup of gruel and limited access to the fire exits.

Jim Earl

Education

Mourning Remembrance

Frank Neuhauser, Winner Of The First National Spelling Bee

Frank Neuhauser, winner of the very first national spelling bee in 1925, is dead. D-E-A-D. Dead.

A family spokesperson said Neuhauser died of Myelodysplastic syndrome, a blood disease so hard to spell, many doctors refuse to cure it.

In 1925 the eleven year-old Neuhauser won first prize by correctly spelling the word "gladiolus." He then promptly returned home to endless schoolyard beatings because he correctly spelled the word "gladiolus."

Jim Earl

First prize included a trip to the White House to meet President Calvin Coolidge, where he quickly learned the word "boring."

Since then, it's been a tradition for contest winners to visit the president in office, including George W. Bush, who still insists "LMNOP" is one letter.

Neuhauser also won $500 in gold and a bicycle, which in today's values would be equal to around $500 in gold and a bicycle.

Neuhauser requested his body be used in a sentence and buried within two minutes and thirty seconds.

Mourning Remembrance

Jim Earl

Exploration

William Irwin Wolff, M.D., Colonoscopy Pioneer

William Irwin Wolff, M.D., originator of the modern colonoscopy procedure now practiced in well-ventilated clinics around the world, has finally seen the murky light at the end of the long, disgusting tunnel.

After graduating from New York University in 1936, Wolff spent years pioneering the field of colonic investigation. Then he became a doctor.

He was the first to develop a safe method for examining the full length of the colon without having to first unhook it from the family Slip N' Slide.

As a result, the relatively unknown surgeon "exploded from behind" to become the "Number One" expert on where "Number Twos" come from.

A dedicated intestinal surgeon, Wolff was known for diving headfirst into each procedure, barely stopping even to catch a breath. Friends say there was no impediment that could keep him from getting his hands dirty.

As president of the New York Surgical Society, Wolff published more than 120 scientific papers. All of them double-ply.

Wolff was a gifted speaker, and his colonoscopy lectures would often leave the audience gripping their seats.

Wolff's procedure inspired several technological advances, the most useful being a wire loop attached to the end of the endoscopic device that doctors now use to remove car keys.

Jim Earl

Wollf's last request was that his sons might continue his legacy taint-free.

Mourning Remembrance

Jim Earl

Fashion

Mourning Remembrance

Don Fisher, Founder of The Gap

Don Fisher, whose company's slogan, "Fall Into the Gap," became synonymous with the dread most people feel when they realize there's no other place in town to buy jeans, fell into another gap recently - this one 4 feet wide and 6 feet deep.

Doctors say Fisher died at his home in San Francisco after a long battle with taste.

Fisher opened the first Gap in 1969 with little more than a pocket full of gumption* and an insatiable desire to measure the unspeakably scandalous distance between the bottom of a man's cuff and the tip of his penis.

Jim Earl

His stores soon caught on and became as commonplace as McDonald's. Even so, you still couldn't get cancer by eating one of Fisher's pants.

An avid art collector, Mr. Fisher was known for his vast collection of paintings - now housed at the Museum of Modern Art in the "Sickening Pastels Wing."

Fisher asked that his body be washed in cold water, cremated on low, and immediately removed from the oven to avoid wrinkling.

* *See Murray Handwerker and Charles Walgreen for more about gumption.*

Mourning Remembrance

E.R. Haggar, Clothing Maker

A world mourns. Eighty-eight-year-old E. R. Haggar, clothing magnate and founder of the Haggar slacks company, died after a long illness where at times it seemed like his life was literally hanging by a thread.

Haggar was found dead at his Dallas home, his tab-waist stretchable trousers expanding for one last time as the inevitable result of rigor mortis.

The son of a Lebanese immigrant, Haggar helped build a family clothing store into a national brand of slacks and shirts that never wrinkled and always smelled weird when you sweat.

Mr. Haggar is survived by his wife of 62 years and lots of remnants.

Jim Earl

Food

Tobin Armstrong, Texas Cattle Rancher

Tobin Armstrong, one of the men most responsible for helping generations of Americans consume dangerous amounts of growth hormones, antibiotics and bovine grease, is now dead meat.

Armstrong would regularly discuss world issues at his 50,000-acre ranch with the likes of Dick Cheney and former President George Bush Sr., while George Jr. would amuse himself by tipping over cows.

The cattle baron's grandfather was a Texas Ranger who became famous for capturing the notorious outlaw John Wesley Hardin. Hardin was reportedly so mean, he once shot a man for snoring while he was shooting a man for snoring.

Armstrong's wife, Anne, once served as advisor to presidents Nixon and Ford. Her most lasting piece of advice? Destroy the tapes and eat more beef.

Armstrong requested his body be hung upside-down in a blood-splattered stainless steel chamber, ceremonially stunned with a retractable metal rod slammed into his forehead, and while still squirming, sent down a conveyor belt to have his tail cut, belly ripped, and hide pulled before a sleep-deprived worker falls into the rendering vat beside him.

Jim Earl

Glen Bell, Founder of Taco Bell

Glen Bell, founder of Taco Bell, has dropped his last chalupa and is now Negra Modeado.

Apparently his heart, stuffed with a delicious blend of three cheeses, refused to pump another ounce of that zesty red sauce.*

Bell opened his first Taco Bell in 1962 using nothing more than some secondhand e coli and absolutely no concept of what real Mexican food tastes like.

In 2007 Taco Bell made headlines after video cameras showed one of their restaurants getting overrun by rats. In its defense, the company said the rats were, "Just trying to get out."

Mourning Remembrance

Bell requested his remains be wrapped in a warm tortilla, stuffed with hearty beans, and grilled to perfection.

* Please see obituary for the Round Table Pizza guy. It's amazing how the lives of complete strangers can somehow interconnect.

Jim Earl

James Conway Sr., Founder of Mister Softee

James Conway, the Mister Softee president who delighted the taste buds of countless children by naming an ice cream cone after a euphemism for impotence, died this weekend of chronic brain freeze.

Conway got his start on St. Patrick's day in 1956 when he served green ice cream to neighbors who were too drunk to notice it was really mold-covered vanilla.

Currently Mister Softee has over 600 trucks on America's streets, an amount that usually doubles whenever Aretha Franklin is on tour.

Even more memorable than the company's soft ice cream is its jingle, first broadcast through a loudspeaker atop a fleet of outdated World War II army trucks purchased in Europe. The original lyrics went like this:

The CREAM-i-est DREAM-i-est SOFT ice CREAM
you GET from MIS-ter SOF-tee.
FOR a re-FRESH-ing de-LIGHT su-PREME
LOOK for MIS-ter SOF-tee....
Achtung Juden! Kommen Sie aus ihre Hauser. Schnell!

Last year, the city of New York and Mister Softee reached a controversial Noise Code agreement under which the trucks may only play the jingles when they are in motion or drowning out a police beating.

The deceased requested his body be frozen, pureed with preservatives and corn syrup, and shot at high pressure through a spiral spout into a flaky waffle coffin.

Jim Earl

H. David Dalquist, Inventor of the Bundt Cake Pan

H. David Dalquist, inventor of the now ubiquitous bundt cake pan, is finally done at the age of 86.

The ailing Dalquist reportedly died of a collapsed lung after someone nearby carelessly slammed an oven door. Doctors attribute his great longevity to preservatives.

The youthful Dalquist grew up with a fascination for metallurgy. And in 1950 he made his first mass-produced bundt cake pan out of aluminum, setting the stage for countless delightful deserts and a whole generation of Alzheimer's induced dementia.

Dalquist requested his remains be sifted, combined with 2 eggs, beaten until light and fluffy, spooned into a greased coffin

Mourning Remembrance

and then cremated at 350 degrees for 45 minutes. Yield should be 10 to 16 servings.

Jim Earl

Hilla Futterman, Expert on Preparing Meals From Weeds

Hilla Futterman, a Los Angeles botanist who for more than 30 years taught classes on how to gather weeds and prepare them for meals, died last week after choking on her neighbor's Johnson Grass.

Naturally equipped with a keen eye for the unappreciated delicacy, Futterman often found her supper popping up through the city's crumbling concrete, which usually turned out to be her dessert.

Her love of weeds made her an authority on such obscure recipes as "dandelion salad," "acorn hash," and "crab grass with essence of Doberman."

Students recalled how her popular classes, which were offered through community colleges, might start at a vacant lot in Marina del Rey and then end up in the "Ragweed Extraction Unit" of the local hospital.

Futterman requested her body be placed on a bed of pickled nutcreeper, sprinkled with spotted goutweed, and topped off with a nice hot frothing glass of pureed stink ivy.

Mourning Remembrance

Murray Handwerker, Owner of Nathan's Famous

Murray Handwerker, who transformed his dad's local hot dog business into something even worse, a national hot dog business, is now completely out of business.

The 89 year-old reportedly died of heart failure after a particularly passionate night spent deboning his meat.

It was way back in 1916 that Murray's father, Nathan, started the little Coney Island hot dog stand with nothing more than a pocket full of gumption* and an acceptable level of rat hair and insect parts.

The stand soon became an American legend, and like Coney Island's amusement parks, its name became virtually synony-

Jim Earl

mous with hot dogs and the sound of people screaming in stomach pain.

Nathan's Famous hot dogs became so popular that President Franklin D. Roosevelt served them to the King and Queen of England on their 1939 visit to America. The story goes that when lunchtime came around the Queen decided she wanted to play a round of Twenty Questions in order to guess what her entrée was going to be, which of course was a delicious Nathan's Famous Hot Dog.

"Off you go then, Elizabeth," said His Majesty starting the game.
"Err… Is it hot and delicious?" the Queen asked.
"Yes, Lizzy," replied the King.
"Oh good," said the Queen, "is it bigger than a breadbox?"
"No," answered the King.
"Oh" she said, "So it's NOT a horse's dick?"

Later in 1945, President Roosevelt had Nathan's hot dogs sent to the Yalta Conference. Within minutes Roosevelt started a fight over, "Who got the Czecho-Coleslaw-Kia," that ended when Stalin reportedly, "slipped Churchill the wiener."

After World War II ended, Handwerker returned home battle weary and tired of the relentless dick jokes. Still the ambitious young man knew the time was ripe to expand the business and give every American the chance to taste his hot, juicy durger.

In a recent interview Nathan's son said that throughout his life the hot dog magnate always ate his frankfurters the same way: "Au naturel." Which probably explains why he was arrested so many times at Yankee Stadium.

Over the decades Handwerker helped create such iconic ad slogans as, "The World's Best Frankfurter," "Nathan's The

Mourning Remembrance

Original Famous," and the memorable, "A Stuck Hot Dog Is Almost Impossible To Dislodge From A Child's Windpipe."

Handwerker requested his remains be run through a grinder, mixed with binders and fillers in a vat, forced through tubes into the small intestine of a sheep, and then placed strategically inside Anthony Weiner's briefs.

See obituaries for Don Fisher and Charles Walgreen. These men also used gumption. Early forms of gumption contained opium and were highly prized by Chinese railroad workers.

Jim Earl

Harriet, the 176-Year-Old Giant Tortoise

Harriet, a 176-year-old tortoise believed to be one of the world's oldest living creatures, died of a heart attack last week after contemplating living another 80 years of her life having to hear about Britney Spears' stupid children.

Harriet was first discovered by Charles Darwin and later owned by Crocodile Hunter Steve Irwin, who later had his heart discovered by a stingray.

Irwin said he considered Harriet a member of his family and could often be seen dangling her over a pit of crocodiles while feeding them live chickens.

According to local legend, the young Harriet was no bigger than a dinner plate when she was taken from the Galapagos

Mourning Remembrance

and given to Queen Victoria for use as one of the world's first reusable diaphragms.

Harriet is the second oldest tortoise ever authenticated. The oldest reportedly died in 1965 after being trampled at a Who concert.

Harriet requested that before she's gutted and stuffed, someone at least clean the diaper rash off her shell from all those humiliating decades spent at the petting zoo.

Jim Earl

Dorothy Harmsen, Co-Founder of Jolly Rancher Candy Company

Dorothy Harmsen, owner of the Jolly Rancher Candy Co. famous for its fruit-flavored candy brick, is dead of a heart attack after trying to pass one.

She and her husband started their candy business back in 1940 with nothing more than a few acres of farmland and a little dream of giving every kid in America a head start on morbid obesity and chronic diabetes.

They began with ice cream but added hard candy 9 years later when they discovered how easy it was to put new labels on 9-year-old ice cream.

At first, they made most of the candies in their barn, selling such confections as "Double Blast Manure Stix," "Blue Raspberry Alfalfa Chews," and the disappointing "Screaming Sour Road Apples."

Known for her immense art collection of paintings and American Indian textiles, Harmsen had recently donated 3,000 pieces to the Denver Art Museum – all of them sticky.

Harmsen requested her body be boiled at 300 degrees, wrapped in clear cellophane foil and twisted at both ends.

Margaret Karcher, Wife of the Founder of Carl's Jr.

Margaret Karcher, the wife of the guy who founded the Carl's Jr. restaurant chain, died this month after enduring 60 years of being known as "the wife of the guy who founded the Carl's Jr. restaurant chain."

She and her husband Carl started the restaurant back in 1941 when Carl, using their Plymouth sedan as collateral, made their first hamburgers out of nothing more than old Bakelite gearshift knobs and mohair upholstery.

The Karchers attributed their success to their strong faith in God. In fact, it was their fascination with the Crucifixion that inspired their favorite Carl's Jr. slogan, "If it doesn't get all over the place, it doesn't belong in your face."

Today Carl's Jr. is proud to sell their Double Six Dollar Burger. At over 1,400 calories, 100 grams of fat, and 2,400 milligrams of salt, it's no wonder Jesus said, "Consider the lilies."

Fans christened it a meal big enough for the horse it was made out of.

Karcher requested her body be dissected into colorful layers, placed neatly on a plate near some fries, and displayed on their website for nutritional content.

Jim Earl

Bill Larson, Founder of Round Table Pizza

Bill Larson, the founder of Round Table Pizza, died Wednesday after his heart, stuffed with a delicious blend of three cheeses, refused to pump another ounce of that zesty red sauce.

Larson's body was found limp and soggy, wedged between two old sofa cushions and a beer-stained copy of *Screw* magazine.

Larson started the restaurant way back in 1959, naming it Round Table after the redwood tables he and his father lovingly built and later made into pizzas.

Over the years, the company became known for making "the last honest pizza." Other slogans included, "I did not have sexual relations with that woman pizza," "Swift Boat veterans for truth pizza," and "Seriously, that's not a wart pizza."

Larson requested his remains be wrapped in aluminum foil and stored in the refrigerator so they can be consumed by his family while watching reruns of *Matlock*.

Mourning Remembrance

Rose Mattus, Co-Founder of Haagen-Dazs

Rose Mattus, who over 40 years ago started Haagen-Dazs ice cream with her husband, died recently after fatally choking on her newest flavor, "Pralines 'N Fur."

It was in way back in 1960 when her husband first came up with the now celebrated name of Haagen-Dazs, two ancient Scandinavian words that when put together mean "diabetic coma."

According to relatives, during the struggling company's early years, Rose would offer free samples in grocery stores. Then she started bringing ice cream.

In 1983, Mattus decided to sell the business to Nestles after a disastrous attempt to compete with Ben & Jerry's with such flavors as "Nutty Nazi Fudge" and "Cookies 'N Death."

Mattus requested her body be crammed into a waffle cone by a bored teenager making four bucks an hour, and then lowered into a bin full of stale, lint-covered M&M's.

Jim Earl

George Molchan, Oscar Mayer Mascot

George Molchan, the lovable little Oscar Mayer mascot who drove the legendary Wienermobile and introduced generations of unsuspecting children to meals of pig snouts, pig lips, spleens, intestines, skeletal muscles, listeria, rubber bands, glass and machine parts, died last week after a long career of just following orders.

Historians say Oscar Mayer created Little Oscar and his Wienermobile in the 1930s to help achieve two important goals. One: inject dangerous amounts of fat into the American diet, and two: make fun of midgets.

The Wienermobile reached the peak of its persuasive powers for selling hotdogs in the 1960s with an estimated 5 million plastic whistles distributed, laying the groundwork for count-

Mourning Remembrance

less choking deaths as well as five new strains of leukemia and colon cancer.

Friends say Molchan loved to drive the funny hot dog on wheels and never tired of appearing at supermarket parking lots just to show off his big wiener.

Molchan eventually became so popular riding around in the strange vehicle, adoring crowds would often surround the oversized novelty sausage in order to receive blessings or hear his sermons against abortion.

Molchan requested his body be sprinkled with sodium nitrite and the ground-up husks of female red beetles in order to make his body appear delicious and fresh, when it would ordinarily appear a putrid gray color.

Jim Earl

Nell Mondy, Potato Expert

Nell Mondy, the Cornell University biochemist who was considered an international expert on the potato, died last month in a New York hospital after a careless nurse left her in a paper bag with a ripened banana.

The famed biochemist and potato aficionado reportedly refused to go on life support, fearing it might turn her into a vegetable.

By the time doctors reached Mondy, startled witnesses say her body had turned soft and brown, and grown at least four eyes.

Attracted by their nutrition, economy, and easy storage, Dr. Mondy first became passionate about potatoes in the 1950s. Soon afterward, she achieved her first orgasm when Mr. Potatohead gave her the "fingerling."

Interesting note: the Incas were the first to cultivate the potato. The Incas also liked to sacrifice virgins to their sun god - a small price to pay for a good plate of fries.

Mondy requested her body be cut into small chunks, boiled, mashed with milk, butter and garlic, and served steaming hot with a big plate of haggis.

Mourning Remembrance

Arnie Morton, Founder of Steakhouse Chain

Arnie Morton, whose string of fancy steakhouses showed the world that colon cancer wasn't just for the poor anymore, died last week after really proving his point.

Morton opened his first restaurant in the 1950s, paving the way for his partnership with Hugh Hefner and their lifelong desire to serve fresh meat to creepy old men.

Morton's first restaurant initially struggled, until the time Frank Sinatra came to eat. From that night on, people from all over flocked to Morton's to taste The Chairman of the Board's favorite entrée, "Scrambled Eggs and Bacon on Warm Breast of Drunken Prostitute."

Morton requested his body be aged two weeks in a cooler until his remains take on a delicious cherry-red color, and then cooked at 1,200 degrees to seal in its juicy goodness.

Jim Earl

Richard Nicholls, Father of the Gilroy Garlic Festival

Richard Nicholls, the man responsible for turning the Gilroy Garlic festival from a small neighborhood party into an internationally known source of intestinal gas and bad breath, has died after years of doctors refusing to go near him.

Under Nicholls' leadership, Gilroy became the Garlic Capital of the World in a bitter competition that beat out the nearby town of Garlic, which had to settle for "Onion Capital of the World."

During the Vietnam War, Nicholls served in the United States Navy, and to this day it's still the only branch of the military that hasn't been attacked by a vampire.

Nicholls requested his body be peeled, cut into manageable pieces, and then forced through small holes in a stainless-steel squeezing device to intensify flavor.

W. Pauline Nicholson, Elvis Presley's Chef

W. Pauline Nicholson, the cook who prepared Elvis Presley's favorite dishes, has left the morgue.

Nicholson died last month of shock after catching the ghost of Elvis stealing food from her refrigerator.

Hired in the mid-1960s as cook and house cleaner, Nicholson quickly grew to affectionately call her boss "Mr. P" long before she even knew what his last name was.

The legendary singer soon grew to love her peanut butter and fried banana concoctions. So much so, he surprised one of the sandwiches with a pink Cadillac.

Nicholson fondly recalled how Elvis would hang out with her in the kitchen at Graceland - in between gulping downers and trying to deport the Beatles.

Her daughter said, "Elvis was like a son to her," adding, "a son who liked to amass huge piles of girls panties in his spookishly weird 23-room mansion."

Nicholson's cooking was so good, the King reportedly found it hard to pass on any of her dishes - until that fatal day in 1977 when he tried to pass her meatloaf.

The deceased requested her body be fried in butter and served to the ghost of Jerry Garcia.

Jim Earl

Joseph L. Owades, Inventor of Light Beer

Joseph L. Owades, the biochemist whose recipe for light beer achieved the impossible feat of making crappy beer even crappier, has finally lost his fizz.

Fresh out of college, Owades got his first job researching for Fleischmann's Yeast. Then he found out Fleischmann was one of his mom's canasta friends and "Yeast" was another thing entirely.

In the 1950s he created the first "diet" beer by discovering an enzyme that destroys fat starches, and in the process, any reason for wanting to drink beer in the first place.

When Miller Brewing Co. bought his process, they marketed the new beer with the familiar slogan, "Tastes great, less fill-

Mourning Remembrance

ing," replacing the less successful, "Hey! You gotta chug twice as much of this crap to get a buzz!"

Over the years Owades wrote more than 40 research papers on beer, all of them supporting the same thesis that he's okay to drive and nobody understands him.

Owades requested his body be brewed into a tasteless yellow liquid and poured directly into the toilet to save time.

Jim Earl

Frank Perdue, Chicken Choker

Frank Perdue, founder of Perdue Chicken, has bought the farm. Police say there's no truth to the rumor his body was found totally battered.

Sixty years ago Perdue took a small backyard egg business and built it into the world's largest source of torture and abuse since the inception of the Catholic Church.

Perdue sold billions of chickens using the folksy slogan, "It takes a tough man to make a tender chicken," which coincidentally was also his favorite pick-up line.

Associates remember his favorite riddle was, "Why did the chicken producer cross the road?" Of course, the answer was always the familiar, "To hire the New York mafia to keep his employees from unionizing."

Perdue is survived by four children, all of whom were raised in a single shed at a density of only 1 square foot of space per child, and bred to grow so fast that they are now on the verge of structural collapse.

The deceased requested his body be hung by the feet from a conveyor belt and dropped into a vat of scalding water while factory employees gleefully toss pieces of his nose and fingers at each other.

Jim Earl

Mitchell Rupe, Convicted Killer Found Too Fat to Hang

Death row inmate Mitchell Rupe, who was once declared by the court to be too fat to execute by hanging, died at the Washington State Penitentiary in Walla Walla after a long battle with a rare liver disease, coincidentally called, "Walla Walla."

After entering prison, Rupe gained 80 pounds by eating approximately 6,000 calories a day, or as he liked to call it, "Fresh meat from Marin."

He was twice sentenced to death. But higher courts overturned his sentence when they found he could barely overturn himself.

In 1994, a federal judge agreed that he was too obese to hang due to the risk of decapitation. But what really swayed his opinion was all those complaints from PETOR, People for the Ethical Treatment of Rope.

According to officials, at the time of his death Rupe weighed 270 pounds, give or take 10 pounds for planted evidence.

Mourning Remembrance

Ruth Siems, Inventor of Stove Top Stuffing

Ruth Siems, the home economist who created Stove Top Stuffing and made it the most popular Thanksgiving leftover since vomit and domestic violence, died last week of a heart attack while "experimenting" with a vibrating turkey baster.

Stove Top Stuffing was first marketed by General Foods in March 1972 and proved to be so popular with the public, Nixon put it on his enemies list.

Friends say Siems first came up with the idea for Stove Top Stuffing while trying to figure out a way to make Thanksgiving more painful.

Jim Earl

Easily prepared in just five minutes, Stove Top stuffing comes in a wide range of flavors, including "turkey," "chicken," "beef," and "smelly uncle Harold."

According to the official United States Patent description, Stove Top Stuffing's secret lay in the crumb size. You see, if the dried bread crumb is too small, adding water makes a soggy mass. Too large, and the result is gravel. In other words, people pay way too much attention to this kind of shit.

Siems requested her remains be toasted, crushed into eraser-sized lumps, and then rammed up the ass of a Butterball turkey so those cheap bastards at General Foods can finally taste the bitter revenge of a woman screwed out of 30 years of patent royalties.

Mourning Remembrance

Donald J. Tyson, Founder of Tyson Foods

Donald J. Tyson, visionary leader of Tyson Foods and instigator of the worst chicken holocaust since Kevin Smith's last barbecue, is now on his way to processing.

The man who made eating chicken almost as safe as living under Chernobyl's concrete containment dome, was found dead in his home, his legs grotesquely pulled apart and looped over his freakishly large breast muscles as if someone had made a cruel wish.

The health department discovered his body buried beneath half a foot of fecal waste, which apparently was scheduled to be cleaned out every 18 months.

As a boy working on his father's chicken ranch, Tyson knew there was something about poultry that he liked. But it wasn't until he enrolled at the University of Arkansas that he truly embraced his love for cock.

Tyson later recalled he could never get enough cock. Though he was partial to white cock, Tyson soon grew to crave black cock as well. "And the bigger the cock the better," he would reportedly exclaim.

In 1952 he married Twilla Womochil, which coincidentally is the sound a chicken makes when you crush its skull with a steel-toed boot.

Under his leadership, the company's revenue increased more than $10 billion. And that's more money than Jesus ever made with his stable of chickens.

Jim Earl

In 2001 the company was charged with using illegal immigrants to work in its chicken processing plants. In his defense, Tyson claimed he was just using them for "nugget filler."

Biographers note Tyson was often compared to fellow Arkansan Sam Walton, primarily because both were huge assholes.

Tyson requested employees stomp, kick, and slam his remains against a wall. But not before hanging him by his feet, cutting off his nose and mockingly playing baseball with his head.

Helen Ullrich, Nutritionist

Helen Ullrich, the celebrated nutritionist who popularized the Food Pyramid and promoted nutritional labels, died of shock this month after learning she was manufactured in a place that handles nuts.

By championing nutritional labels and the Food Pyramid, Ullrich made it easier for Americans to understand what they were eating, and in the process, stuff themselves with the kind of crap that makes this country the stupidest, fattest place on earth.

Ullrich introduced the Food Pyramid in 1988 after rejecting such earlier prototypes as the Cheese Ziggurat, the Tripe Tent, and the Quasi-Regular Dodecahedron of Pork.

Ullrich requested her remains be packaged with all her ingredients clearly marked on the casket.

Jim Earl

Michael Vale, Star of 100 Dunkin' Donuts Commercials

Michael Vale, who for 15 years played Fred the Baker in over 100 Dunkin Donuts commercials, was found dead in his apartment, his eyes glazed, body twisted, and stomach swollen with a rich, tangy lemon filling.

Vale was forced to retire in 1997 when skeptical fans questioned whether someone could actually work that long at a donut shop without getting killed by a crack dealer.

Police officers were such a huge fan of Vale, they used to pull him over on the highway just to get an autograph, and if they were lucky, get a taste of his delicious donut hole.

Mourning Remembrance

When he was once asked by *Entertainment Weekly* if he had ever actually made donuts, Vale reportedly crouched down, strained his face and quipped, "I'm making one now, eraygh!" He was never asked for an interview again.

The deceased requested his body be dunked halfway into a giant vat of Sanka and then dropped from a freeway overpass onto somebody's windshield as a joke.

Jim Earl

Heroism

Mourning Remembrance

Wesley Hill, Niagara Falls Rescuer

Wesley Hill, the man who helped rescue dozens of people from the treacherous Niagara Falls, was found dead last week in a barrel, apparently the victim of his drinking buddies' misguided attempt to act out an old bar joke.

Hill was the last remaining member of a family whose business it was to rescue people too dumb to notice the river actually had a bridge going across it.

Tragically, Hill's brother was killed in the 1950s while attempting to go over Niagara Falls in a barrel made out of Hula Hoops and pieces of James Dean's Porsche Spyder.

Jim Earl

In his 20s, Hill advised the crew working on the film *Niagara*. It was his job to bring Marilyn Monroe her coffee, donuts, and whenever she was low, fresh hangover vomit.

Wesley Hill's father was Red Hill, a legendary river man who recovered more than 300 bodies from Niagara Falls. All, coincidentally, strangled and nude. Strange, nobody ever asked Red about that.

Hill requested he be buried in a place where nobody can ever find him and put him in a barrel.

Mourning Remembrance

Jim Earl

Invention

Samuel Alderson, Crash Test Dummy Inventor

Samuel Alderson, inventor of crash test dummies that are used to make cars, parachutes and other devices safer, was found dead last week after two disgruntled dummies rammed his body through the windshield of a 1964 Chevy Corvair.

Family members reassured themselves with the knowledge that Alderson's death will, quote, "be an accurate predictor of what may generally happen in the field when 90-year-old skin panels and internal organs eventually lose their tensile strength."

Alderson's invention set the industry standard. But, sadly, his reputation took a blow in recent times when he insisted his employees use the dummies for his web site to conduct what he called "important fondle tests."

Jim Earl

A pioneer in his field, Alderson was the first to measure the effects of a human spinal column crashing into a tree by making his test dummies go for beer runs with Leif Garret.

George C. Ballas Sr., Inventor Of The Weed Eater

George C. Ballas Sr., a Houston developer who invented the Weed Eater, is now being eaten by weeds.

Ballas said he got the idea for his machine after watching spinning brushes at a local car wash. He wondered if the same principle that inspired Americans to underpay migrants to wash their cars could also inspire them to underpay migrants to piss off the neighbors with noise and choking exhaust fumes.

Ballas soon began experimenting by poking holes in a tin can with fishing wire and attaching it to a rotary lawn edger. Seven maimed cats later, the "Pussy Eater" was born. But it wasn't until someone suggested he use it on weeds that his invention really took off.

Ballas was the grandfather of *Dancing With The Stars* dancer Mark Ballas. Mark got the idea to become a dancer after watching a weed eater make everyone in his family so filthy rich they'd never have to worry about getting a real job.

Ballas requested his remains be cremated and the ashes scattered in front of a leaf blower.

Jim Earl

John Barron, Inventor of The ATM

John Barron, a Scotsman who over forty years ago invented the automated teller machine, is out of cash.

Witnesses say he died after an irate customer rammed a crowbar into his mouth-slot after he refused to dispense fifty dollars.

News of his death couldn't be confirmed until four days after Barron was deposited at the morgue because the bank said they had to put a hold on his corpse.

Barron said he came up with the idea for ATMs after being locked out of his bank. He also said his invention was inspired by candy vending machines. Which begs the question: Which story is it, asshole?

Mourning Remembrance

In a recent interview, the 84 year-old Scottish inventor recalled how the original machines were so primitive, they only dispensed haggis.

Interesting factoids:

-The world's highest ATM is located in Tibet at 5,000 meters.

-The world's lowest ATM is located 400 meters below sea level near the Dead Sea.

-And the world's stickiest is in Amsterdam. It's literally packed with semen.

Barron requested his body be dried and molded into a hard protective case containing four trays of twenty-dollar bills, then placed in any dark area where people may gather to get robbed or kidnapped.

Jim Earl

Rebecca Carranza, Inventor of the Tortilla Chip

Rebecca Web Carranza, acknowledged creator of the first tortilla chip, died of a heart attack last month after accidentally eating a priceless plate of nachos in the shape of the Virgin Mary.

Witnesses say her body was found cracked and soggy, face down in a half-eaten bowl of picante sauce and surrounded by a bunch of teenage boys too insecure to leave the snack table and go mingle with the girls standing by the keg.

Relatives say there's no truth to the rumor she died after breaking her hip on an unusually heavy chunk of guacamole.

Carranza's Los Angeles tortilla shop was the favorite of many celebrities. Eddie "Rochester" Anderson, who played Jack

Benny's valet on radio and television, would often buy a bag of her chips and then swallow them whole to create his horribly painful voice.

Carranza requested her remains be passed around at a party and then stored in an airtight, plastic bag for freshness.

Jim Earl

Samuel T. Cohen, Inventor of The Neutron Bomb

Samuel T. Cohen, inventor of the neutron bomb, died in his home recently after straining for days on what he tragically dubbed "my clam sausage ordnance."

Paramedics were shocked to find his internal organs had completely disintegrated, leaving the surrounding skin remarkably intact.

Cohen developed his neutron bomb in the 1950s at the request of the government, who needed a way to kill enemy troops without harming buildings housing the world's precious reserves of Hula Hoops.

Mr. Cohen was married twice. His first marriage ended in divorce in 1952 after his wife caught him in bed with Fat Man and Little Boy.

His bomb's main appeal was its lethal output of tiny neutral particles that can pass through buildings without notice. He dubbed these particles "Walter Mondales."

Soviet Premier Nikita Khrushchev called Cohen's invention the ultimate capitalist weapon, built, "to kill a man in such a way that his suit will not be stained with blood, in order to appropriate the suit." He then ruined the moment by banging his shoe on a table.

In 1981 President Ronald Reagan ordered 700 neutron warheads built to oppose the Soviet Union, and even had several of them tested on his brain.

Years later, President George H. W. Bush ordered the massive stockpile disarmed and stored safely inside his wife's cast iron womb.

Cohen requested his body be mistakenly dropped on an Iraqi wedding celebration.

Jim Earl

Harry Wesley Coover Jr., Inventor of Super Glue

After a prolonged illness, Harry Wesley Coover Jr., inventor of Super Glue, is now Super Dead.

Doctors fought bravely throughout his illness to reduce cranial swelling but no matter how hard they tried, they could never get his cap off.

Before long, they knew he only had a matter of days – mainly because his face was so pasty.

Coover's wife was the first to discover the body, so naturally she became totally unglued.

A spokesman denied rumors he was discovered alone in his bedroom, "lying next to a large stack of stroke mags with his hand stuck to his Coover."

The inventor was once described as, "one of the true legends of the adhesive industry." Of course, this was immediately followed by derisive laughter.

Legend has it Coover invented Super Glue in 1951 after carelessly dropping a used pair of Walter Brennan's underwear into a Reese's Peanut Butter Cup.

The original mixture consisted of monomers of Methyl-2-cyanoacrylate molecules with a molecular weight equal to or greater than 111.1. Whew, is it just me or are you gettin' horny?

Over the years Coover's Super Glue has been used to repair millions of everyday items, but sadly, it can never mend a broken heart.

Mourning Remembrance

At his eulogy, Coover's children recounted many fond memories growing up in a happy home where the walls were always covered with patches of torn human skin.

Friends found the memorial very enjoyable. And when it came time to bury him, everybody just had to stick around.

Coover requested his remains be placed in a brown paper bag so neighborhood teens can use it for "kicks."

Jim Earl

Bertram Given, Inventor of the Garbage Disposal

Bertram F. Given, who in 1945 invented the Waste King garbage disposal, passed away this month after 60 years of watching his work go down the drain.

Given died tragically while personally demonstrating his ill-conceived In-Trojan-Ator, a powerful chopping-suction device used to collect and pulverize discarded condoms at the bottom of hot tubs.

Given first came up with the idea for the garbage disposal while seeking a better way for children to maim themselves while searching the sink-pipe for their father's lost Rolex.

Always hip to his times, Given once told reporters in 1966, "What women want in the kitchen is Automation, Cleanability, Interchangeability, and Durability," or ACID.

The deceased requested his remains be chopped into very small pieces with stainless steel blades driven by a 2-horsepower, high-torque insulated electric motor so they can safely flow through the plumbing without clogging it.

Mourning Remembrance

Ronald Howes, Inventor of the Easy-Bake Oven

Ronald Howes, inventor of Kenner's Easy-Bake oven, finally burst an artery last week after waiting three aggravating months for a 30-watt bulb to cook his goddamn brownie.

Friends say the toy oven inventor lived a long, productive life before dying at 83 - degrees.

Howes first got the idea for his invention in 1963 after realizing that any nation dumb enough to swallow the lone gunman theory was more than willing to let their children be swindled by a cheap plastic box with a light bulb in it.

Howes' first job at Kenner Toys was to remove potentially poisonous chemicals from cans of Play-Doh and inject them into the sad, withered teats of Milky The Marvelous Milking Cow.

Howes also invented Kenner's Easy-Tan, where kids could create their own tans simply by mixing water with packets of John Boehner's skin flakes.

Later, he helped perfect the Spirograph. A toy that used a set of precision plastic gears, rings and triangles to geometrically depict the downward spiral of Spiro Agnew's political career.

In 2008, almost 1 million Easy-Bake Ovens had to be recalled for safety reasons. Apparently children were suffering serious lacerations when they tried to force the family cat into the broiler.

Howes requested his body be inserted into the side of the local crematorium, pushed out a slot at the other end, and consumed by a generation of kids vainly seeking to fill the bottomless void of a loveless childhood.

Jim Earl

Robert Kearns, Inventor of Intermittent Wipers

Robert W. Kearns, beloved inventor of the intermittent rotating rubber-scraper mechanism responsible for squeegeeing rain off the windshields of millions of automobiles, was found dead at his home, completely wiped out.

By the time paramedics arrived, Kearns' aged, cracked, and grit-filled body had already left unsightly streaks all over the house.

During the last few days of Kearns' debilitating illness, witnesses say the inventor could barely pivot his arms back and forth long enough to wipe himself.

Though he was married with six children, there is some evidence in earlier years that Kearns liked to swing his blade both ways.

There's a lot more to this man's life, but those are about all the cheap jokes I could come up with using the words "blade" "swing" and "wipe."

Jim Earl

Richard LaMotta, Creator of the Chipwich Ice Cream Sandwich

Richard LaMotta, inventor of the Chipwich, a cold slab of vanilla sandwiched between two chunky chocolate-chip cookies, is now freezing his chips off on a cold slab of concrete.

Friends say there's no truth to the rumor his heart gave out at the Two-Potato Bar in the West Village after attempting to squeeze himself between two chunky men to create a "Manwich."

LaMotta debuted his invention on the streets of New York in 1982. And within two weeks, he was selling over 40,000 Chipwiches a day, mostly to the ghost of Elvis.

At one point, Chipwiches became so popular that Mayor Ed Koch agreed to pose for a famous photo of himself biting into a one. Eight years later a New York cop raped Abner Louima with a broom stick. Coincidence? You be the judge.

There were many Chipwich imitations on the market, but none ever seemed to catch the public's fancy. They included names like "Chilly Chips," "Chips 'n' Chips," and the hugely unsuccessful, "Two Slabs of Crud Surrounding a Lump of Shit - With Limen."

Richard was a cousin of boxing champ Jake LaMotta, whose love for the creamy concoction became so intense, he once even accused Richard of fucking his Chipwich.

LaMotta requested his melted inside parts be siphoned off by British Petroleum in order to avert any more damage to the Gulf.

Mourning Remembrance

Milton Levine, Inventor of The Ant Farm

Milton Levine, creator of the popular Ant Farm that gave countless children a personal look into the underground lives of insects, is now giving countless ants a personal look into his gallbladder.

Levine died after falling asleep underneath a giant magnifying glass he was building for the time when giant mutant ants will most certainly attack us from outer space.

When family members discovered his body, they were shocked to find Levine's wallet and Rolex had been stolen by dreaded "crack ants."

Levine became fascinated by ants in his childhood, and pledged to someday honor the magnificent creatures' 22,000

Jim Earl

species and 130 million years of earthly existence by trapping them inside a plastic box with a miniature windmill.

His first Ant Farms in the 1950s featured a green plastic frame with a whimsical farm scene, including a traveling salesman ant that would end up sleeping with the farmer's daughter ant.

Levine's subsequent inventions in the 1960s never quite hit it off as big. Like the Spahn Ant Ranch, where hippie ants would vie for the affection of a mesmerizing bearded ant with connections to Dennis Wilson.

Levine requested his remains be filled with special semitransparent gel to provide moisture and egg-laying structures, and then buried in Antietam National Cemetery.

Mourning Remembrance

Philip Morrison, A-Bomb Inventor

Philip Morrison, one of the main inventors of the atomic bomb, died last week after living much longer than his calculated half-life.

A group leader in the Manhattan Project, Morrison helped launch the age of nuclear weapons, and even more insidiously, the subsequent era of plastic pocket protectors.

After the war, Morrison became a leader in the search for intelligent life in the universe and the most efficient ways to destroy them with radiation.

The deceased, who witnessed the explosion of the first atomic bomb in New Mexico, requested his irradiated body be given to the United Way and used for the next 300 years as a nightlight in local rest homes.

Jim Earl

Elwood Perry, Maker of a Fishing Lure

Elwood Perry, who in 1946 invented the Spoonplug fishing lure loved by the millions of fishing enthusiasts, is now chum.

The 90-year-old Perry reportedly died while testing his latest invention, the "toaster-oven lure."

On July 24, 1954 before dozens of witnesses, Perry used his Spoonplug 30 times to land 30 bass, setting a new world record. Not for fishing, but for holding the attention of dozens of people while doing something that boring.

During his career, Perry discovered two profound truths about outdoor sporting:

One: Always drag a lure so it bounces off the bottom.

Mourning Remembrance

Two: Never *ever* ask Ned Beaty about that rape scene in *Deliverance*.

Perry requested his body be folded in two, impaled on a hook, and dragged along the bottom of a pond so fish could freely nibble on his jig wobbler.

Jim Earl

Robert Rich, Inventor of Nondairy Whipping

Robert Rich, inventor of nondairy whipped topping, died last month after a short illness creamed him.

Rich's nondairy products were the result of the food shortages during World War II, when large amounts of milk products were sent overseas to help make German supply routs soggy.

Unlike real cream, Rich's "cream" could be safely stored for over a year without losing its ability to turn a generation of Americans into doughy slugs who would actually sit through an episode of *Ozzie and Harriet*.

Rich is survived by his beloved wife, who like his whipped topping, required little-or-no prep-time and spread easily.

Mourning Remembrance

Gerry Thomas, Inventor of the TV Dinner

Gerry Thomas, the man who perfected the concept of putting dangerous amounts of fat, sodium, and MSG into aluminum trays and freezing them so a whole generation of children could grow up insane in front of the television, died last month after choking on a Swanson Hungry Man.

Witnesses say when doctors reached him, Thomas was warm on the outside but still frozen solid in the middle.

Thomas's original aluminum TV Dinner tray can now be seen in the Smithsonian Institution next to a diorama of the first domestic beating it caused.

Thomas was honored for his invention in 1999 when he was asked to press his hands and TV tray into the cement outside

Jim Earl

Grauman's Chinese Theatre. Paramedics had to be called when Thomas mistook the lukewarm, half-congealed mixture for a pile of Swanson's Potatoes & Beef Gravy.

The deceased requested his remains be crammed into a metal tray with the foil pealed back, and each organ sealed in a separate compartment to avoid mixing any liver gravy with his brain noodles.

Mourning Remembrance

Arch West, Creator of Doritos

Arch West, who 50 years ago took a warehouse full of cornmeal, MSG, and pork excretions, and turned it into the world's first edible Superfund site, is now covered with an orange, crusty-coating of crispy death.

Doctors say dying was the only natural thing he did his whole life.

A company spokesperson denied West died while testing his latest creation, "Double-Fisted Kettle Cooked Carburetor-Cleaner Flavored Chips With Tangy Asbestos."

Food historians say you can find vintage examples of the first Doritos ever manufactured still moldering inside Paul Sorvino's intestinal gas pockets.

A humble man by nature, West often declined to take full credit for Doritos' inception in 1961, instead giving most of it to NASA's helpful staff of Nazi chemists.

In 2008, the company launched "out-of-this-world," a promotion in which they beamed a Doritos ad into a planetary system 42 light years away. Their ultimate goal? To dissuade aliens from ever using us as their food source.

The family plans on tossing some Doritos over West's urn before burying him, but not until they do marketing research on 5,000 other graves.

Jim Earl

Morrie Yohai, Inventor of the Cheez Doodle

Morrie Yohai, inventor of the Cheez Doodle, is now Cheez Deadle.

Doctors say his heart gave out after hours of straining through a particularly "difficult doodle."

By the time paramedics found his body, it was already caked with a delicious yellow powder and puffed to a delightful crunchy consistency. Plus he had cancer.

Yohai was proud of his invention, yet his family says he was more interested in pursuing Jewish mysticism.
As we all know, according to the Zohar, study of the Torah can only proceed along these three methods:

Peshat: Directly interpreting meaning.
Remez: Interpreting meaning through allegories.
and
Derash: Interpreting meaning by boiling it in vats, extruding it under high pressure through a narrow hole, and coating it with fake cheese. Plus he had cancer.

Yohai requested his body be ground up with the body of the guy who invented Cheez Wiz and used as a sexual lubricant for turtles.

Jim Earl

Mike Yurosek, Inventor of 'Baby' Carrots

Mike Yurosek, the inventor of those peeled "baby" carrots used around the world by heroin addicts trying to kick the habit, died last week after chomping down on his own niblet.

It was in 1986 when Yurosek perfected a way to take misshapen and broken carrots that would ordinarily be discarded, and basically make a huge fortune out of trash.

The miniaturized vegetable boosted carrot sales by 35 percent, inspiring Yurosek to further increase profits by miniaturizing wages.

Many less-successful Yurosek innovations followed, including "Baby, Baby Peas," "Zuchinni-Weenies," and the puzzling "Mushroom-Shaped Mushrooms."

Thanks to Yurosek, Americans today are eating a lot more carrots than their parents did. They're also eating a lot more insect parts and rat droppings, so I guess things have a way of balancing themselves out.

Yurosek was an active volunteer at religious organizations and could often be seen whittling a knobby, misshapen crucifix into bite-sized pieces.

The deceased requested his body be dismembered, shaped into 2-inch segments, and pumped through pipes into a peeling tank for final polishing.

Jim Earl

Literary

Mourning Remembrance

Shelby Foote, Civil War Historian and Novelist

"Shelby Foote, the southern historian who in the 1990 Ken Burns Civil War documentary touched the hearts of millions of Americans with his thick, Memphis drawl, died of a heart attack after tragically realizing no one could ever understand a single word he was saying."
    ---George Templeton Strong.

"The hit series turned Mr. Foote into a television star. And at one point, he was getting at least 20 calls a day from Civil War fans asking him to explain what 'goober peas' were."
    ---Elizabeth Cady Stanton.

"Critics say Foote deliberately embellished the epic nature of battles in order to play down the evils of slavery and make Southern soldiers seem more heroic. While others say any

price was worth paying just to take their attention away from Ken Burns' haircut."
    ---Mary Boykin Chestnut

"Mr. Foote asked that a black and white photograph be taken of his remains so Ken Burns could slowly 'pan and zoom' over it for ten and a half hours."
    ---Elisha Hunt Rhodes.

Mourning Remembrance

Dale Messick, Creator of 'Brenda Starr' Reporter

Dale Messick, the pioneering comic book artist who created the chic, red-haired reporter Brenda Starr, died last week after suffering critical circulation problems in over 20 important markets.

When the comic strip started in 1940, Brenda had everything a woman could dream of: brains, beauty, and up to one-half the salary of her male co-workers.

Messick passed the strip on for other artists to draw in 1980, 50 years after it stopped being fashionable to say things like, "Jeepers, that's some jalopy," and "Say, you're one swell egg."

Near the end of her life, Messick often complained she didn't like the way the later versions of Brenda Starr looked. Sadly, no one had the heart to tell her she was reading *Fred Basset*.

Jim Earl

Lyle Stuart, Controversial Book Publisher

Lyle Stuart, the infamous literary figure whose company published *The Anarchist Cookbook*, died of a heart attack at his home in Fort Lee, coincidentally just after publishing the controversial volume, *How to Make Your Dad Die of a Heart Attack At His Home in Fort Lee*.

In the 1960s, Stuart fueled the popularity of sex-related books by publishing *The Sensuous Woman* and *The Sensuous Man*, followed quickly by *The Disinterested Lesbian*, *The Sexless Egg-Shaped Person*, and *The Creepy Guy Always Standing Just Outside the Perimeter Of Your Property*.

Stuart launched his company in 1956 with an $8,000 libel settlement he won against gossip columnist Walter Winchell, who reportedly told him, "Close your yap, ya dumb mug. And deal back the mazuma before I stuff that mud pipe down your mush."

Stuart went on to publish *The Anarchist Cookbook* in 1970 after first believing it was just a guide to making egg salad without mustard.

Stuart requested his remains be buried with a copy of his latest publication, *How to Blow Up Heaven*.

Mourning Remembrance

Max Velthuijs, Author of Popular Children's Books

Max Velthuijs, the beloved Dutch author and illustrator of children's stories featuring the curious and trusting character, Frog, has croaked.

Offering life parables to children of three years and older, Velthuijs' popular Frog character struggled with bitter cold in the story *Frog in Winter*, confronted a scary noise in *Frog Is Frightened*, and finally discovered his roots in the acclaimed *Frog Eats His Young*.

Velthuijs' first big success was the story *Frog in Love* in which Frog is smitten with a Duck. The story became so popular, that the Dutch author received the prestigious Hans Christian Andersen Medal for Most Disturbing Fetish of 1989.

Jim Earl

Velthuijs' long awaited masterpiece, a moody tome capturing the protean quality of dreams and shattering the conventions of the waking mind, *Froggigan's Wake*, remained unfinished at the time of his death.

Velthuijs requested his ashes be scattered nowhere near the scores of penis-shaped water fountains situated throughout Amsterdam.

Mourning Remembrance

Jim Earl

Medicine

Daniel Ruge, President Reagan's White House Physician

Daniel Ruge, the man chosen to be Ronald Reagan's White House physician during his first term as president, has died from a ruptured gipper.

Early in his career, Ruge practiced medicine with First Lady Nancy Reagan's stepfather, who taught him the family secrets of pre-death facial embalming.

After the 1981 assassination attempt on Reagan, Ruge remained at Reagan's side and nursed him back to health with the president's favorite vegetable dish: Baked Catsup.

Jim Earl

Ruge never stayed for the second term. He was asked to leave in 1984 after he gave the president a battery of diagnostic tests which declared him brain dead.

Dr. Ruge requested his body be dug up every year, examined by doctors, and declared fit enough to serve public office.

Jack Scholl, Foot-Care Pioneer

Jack E. Scholl, head of the pioneering foot-care company Dr. Scholl's, finally got the boot last week after stubbing his big toe on a little thing called "death."

Horrified loved ones discovered Scholl's body at his Illinois home, where according to the coroner, it had spent the last two weeks "gellin'."

Scholl's late uncle began the legendary business back in 1904 in what would become a lifelong quest to keep people from looking down on feet.

As a producer of the world's finest comfort footwear, Scholl always prided himself with being surrounded by plenty of "high-priced hose."

Relatives say Scholl requested he be shoe-horned into a casket two sizes too small for his body.

Jim Earl

Charles Socarides, the Psychiatrist Who Said Gays Could Become Straight.

Dr. Charles W. Socarides, a psychiatrist/psychoanalyst who spent his career arguing that homosexuality was a curable disease, is dead of heart failure after realizing his favorite part in Ben Hur between Charlton Heston and Stephen Boyd is probably the gayest scene anyone ever put in a movie.

In the 1960s, his theory that gays were victims of a treatable mental illness engendered international reaction, mostly in the form of withering sarcasm and flamboyantly obscene gestures.

With all the scorn, he still stuck to his beliefs - even when the American Psychiatric Association removed homosexuality from its list of mental disorders in 1973 and replaced it with "Disco Fever."

Socarides published at least 11 books throughout his career, including *The Overt Homosexual*, 1995's *Homosexuality: A Freedom Too Far*, and the best-selling *Okay, My Son is Gay. I Can Explain This, Really. Hear Me Out*.

Socarides is survived by three divorced wives, four children and lots of unopened closets.

William G. Speed, Migraine Expert

William G. Speed, who for the last 60 years was considered the world's expert on migraine headaches, has died after a lifetime of being a chronic pain in the ass.

Born in Baltimore, Dr. Speed knew from any early age that he wanted to become a doctor, mainly because that might get him out of Baltimore.

While a student at Trinity College, Speed first became interested in migraines after meeting countless women who used them as an excuse not to have sex with him.

Today migraines are defined as severe headaches often accompanied by nausea and vomiting, symptoms usually associated with learning that Seth Rogen just landed another romantic lead role.

The deceased requested his body be placed under a hot shower, then a cold one, then a hot one, then a cold one, then a hot one. And then just left alone for a while, dammit.

Jim Earl

Leo Sternbach, Creator of Valium

Leo Sternbach, a research chemist responsible for developing the most addictive muscle relaxant since Kaopectate, is now dead calm.

At the height of Valium's popularity in 1978, Sternbach's company sold over 2 billion tablets evenly split between Liz Taylor and Liza Minnelli.

Always the hands-on technician, Sternbach once tried Valium. He reported its only side-effects were increased drowsiness followed by the urge to marry Gerald Ford.

For most patients, the drug imparts a mild euphoria. But that wears off once you wake up to find you've killed your grunge-rock husband with a shotgun.

In 2003 members of the pharmaceutical industry celebrated the 40th anniversary of Valium by lying down on the living room floor, drooling on their shirts, and then slowly watching a lit cigarette burn the drapes.

Sternbach requested his body be combined with the bodies of other drug inventors to create a dangerously erotic synergistic reaction.

Jim Earl

Military

Mourning Remembrance

Edward N. Hall, Father of the Minuteman Missile

Colonel Ed Hall, widely considered by most fans of mutually assured destruction to be the father of the Minuteman ICBM, died recently when one of his missiles refused to exit the silo after four painful hours of straining on the toilet.

His solid-fuel rocket technology has also been used in such famous U.S. missiles as the Polaris and the Titan III, as well as the Space Shuttle Challenger. And we all know how well that worked out.

After graduating with a degree in chemical engineering at City College of New York, Hall couldn't find a job because of the economy. It was then he first decided to devote the rest of his life perfecting ways to send dynamite through the air to blow up civilians.

Jim Earl

After winning numerous awards throughout his career, he was made a member of the Hall of Fame at the U.S. Air Force Space Command – primarily for being the only guy there who wasn't an ex-Nazi.

Hall requested his remains be buried in 500 holes around Wyoming, Montana and North Dakota.

Samuel Koster, General Charged in My Lai Massacre

General Samuel W. Koster, the highest-ranking officer in the Vietnam War to face punishment for his connection with the My Lai massacre, has been demoted from life.

Koster was in command of the Army's largest division on March 16, 1968, when his troops slaughtered 500 women, children and old men in a South Vietnamese village now called "Little Wal-Mart."

Koster flew over the village during the massacre, and was never on the ground. But afterwards he claimed only about 20 civilians had died, largely in what he called, "careless bathtub accidents."

Survivors include his wife, five children, and 15 grandchildren, who funny enough, have never been burned alive in their huts and buried in a mass grave.

Jim Earl

Bruce Peterson, the Real "Six Million Dollar Man"

Former NASA test pilot Bruce Peterson, whose violent crash became the basis for an even bigger disaster, the 1970s TV series *Six Million Dollar Man*, is now two dollars worth of dust inside a six-dollar coffin.

Peterson apparently died of heart failure after having to endure 30 years of phone calls from a confused Farrah Fawcett.

Peterson crashed in the M2-F2, a wingless "lifting body" aircraft that led to the development of the space shuttle, a winged "lifting body" aircraft that led to the development of an endless series of tasteless Challenger jokes.

Mourning Remembrance

Actual film footage of Peterson's famous crash was seen in the opening credits of the TV series, followed by the now classic line, "Whoops, wrong button!"

Peterson is survived by two children and the wreckage of Lee Majors' career.

Jim Earl

Albert L. Weimorts, Designer of Big Bombs

Albert L. Weimorts, a civilian engineer who designed some of the biggest conventional bombs ever made, is dead after his flaps refused to open while attempting to drop a load of potato salad.

Weimorts developed the enormous "Bunker Buster" bombs of the first Iraq War, which were primarily used to "bust" the United States economy.

Weimorts' most powerful bomb was called the "Massive Ordnance Air Blast," a nickname inspired by the sound Barbara Bush makes after eating pork.

Mr. Weimorts was also project engineer for cluster bombs that had a production rate of eight million bomblets a month during the Vietnam War. So that's a lot to be proud of, right?

Weimorts requested his body be encased in two tons of hardened steel and dropped at high altitude onto the impregnable concrete porn bunker at Neverland Ranch.

General William Westmoreland, Vietnam War General

William Westmoreland, commanding general for the U.S. during the Vietnam War, has finally seen the light at the end of the tunnel.

During the 1960s, the highly disciplined and strong-willed Westmoreland represented the ideal image of an American military leader. Unfortunately that American military leader was George Custer.

Born to upper class parents in South Carolina, Westmoreland was able to take the lessons learned from his state's pointlessly tragic losses during the Civil War, and completely ignore them during the Vietnam War.

Jim Earl

According to one biographer, Westmoreland loved ice cream and liked to drink two gin and tonics every night. A habit that not only explains him seeing a light at the end of a tunnel, but throwing up in one as well.

The deceased requested his body be cremated and his ashes dropped into a humiliating quagmire.

Mourning Remembrance

Jim Earl

Music

Mourning Remembrance

James Griffin, Co-Founder of the Band Bread

Baby I'm-A Dead.

This week the music world received word that James Griffin, founding member of the soft-rock group Bread, is toast. In a statement released today to hopeful fans, Griffin's manager said there was no truth to the rumor he's risen. But I guess that news is pretty stale by now.

Never one to loaf, Griffin helped form Bread in 1968. And after they released the hits "Make It With You" and "Baby I'm-a Want You," Bread was on a roll. Any way you sliced it, Bread was hot. And Bread made a lot of dough.

Griffin had been in good health until last week when doctors labeled his condition as "crummy." When loved-ones discov-

Jim Earl

ered his body, witnesses say the former lead singer of Bread was crusty and completely riddled with fungus. Nothing could be saved, not even the heels.

Griffin requested his body be interned at the family cemetery, sandwiched between two graves.

Mourning Remembrance

Eric Griffiths, Guitarist for the Quarrymen.

Eric Griffiths, a guitarist who played alongside Paul McCartney and George Harrison in John Lennon's high school band The Quarrymen, is now getting deader all the time. He was 64.

Asked to comment on the touching coincidence that his former band mate passed away "when he was 64," a reference to the hit song on the Sergeant Peppers album, Sir Paul McCartney answered, "Eric who?"

When the 11-year-old Griffiths first met John Lennon in high school, he quickly discovered he shared Lennon's enthusiasm for quote, "music, smoking, and shrill, meddling girlfriends with a penchant for bad conceptual art."

Eric's talent and versatility apparently had such an impact on Lennon and McCartney, that when George Harrison joined the group in 1958, Eric was asked to switch to bass. In another band.

Eric later left the group to become a sailor in the British merchant navy. It was during one of his many long voyages at sea when he and his crew mates first heard "Please Please Me," not the Beatles' first No. 1 hit, but a request from his sadistic cabin master.

Fans say Griffiths is now up in heaven getting thrown out of Stu Sutcliffe's band.

Jim Earl

Eugene Landy, Brian Wilson's 24-Hour A Day Therapist

"Lets start dying now, everybody's learning how, come to a big funeral with me."

Eugene Landy, the psychotherapist who for almost two decades was responsible for wheeling out Brian Wilson's drug-soaked, whale-sized body to the amusement and horror of countless ripped-off Beach Boys fans, died last month after hysterically laughing himself to the bank one too many times.

Many believe Landy was responsible for Wilson's successful comeback in the early 1980s after the singer had spent years being stuck in the doorway of a giant walk-in meat freezer.

Landy's treatment included padlocking the refrigerator, forcing Wilson to exercise, and on mornings when he wouldn't get up, shocking Brian out of bed with videos of Mike Love's creepy dancing.

By 1990, Landy had wormed himself into Wilson's life so much that he was acting as his business partner, and at one point, even took over his father's former job of beating him on the head with a two-by-four.

Landy requested his body keep constant vigil over Brian Wilson in order to make sure he never teams up again with Charlie Manson, or worse, Van Dyke Parks.

Robert Moog, Creator of the Moog Synthesizer

Robert Moog, inventor of the music synthesizer that bares his name, and the man most responsible for destroying pop music, has died of shame after actually hearing Paul McCartney's "Maxwell's Silver Hammer" for the first time.

The Moog was first heard in 1967 on a Monkees album. The Monkees later went down in history as the first pop group to ever be accused of not performing their own songs with instruments that weren't real.

Music historians believe Moog will best be remembered as the man who made 8-track tapes sound even worse.

Family members were able to console themselves with the thought that Moog's now up in Heaven, playing an artificial harp.

Jim Earl

Lucy Vodden, Music Victim

Lucy Vodden, the girl who inspired the Beatles' song "Lucy in the Sky With Diamonds," is now "Lucy in the Ground with Ants."

Her death was announced forty years to the day after Yoko killed *The White Album*.

Back in 1967, Vodden was a schoolmate of John Lennon's son, Julian, who brought home a drawing and called it "Lucy in the Sky with Diamonds." But Lennon didn't use it as inspiration for his psychedelic masterpiece until Eric Clapton brought home a bag and called it "heroin."

Two years later, history was made again when Julian brought home a drawing of a turd and called it "Maxwell's Silver Hammer."

Friends and family can take comfort in the fact that she outlived Julian Lennon's career.

Mourning Remembrance

Jim Earl

Pioneers

Mourning Remembrance

John Diebold, Computer Visionary

John Diebold, the great futurist whose persistent promotion of computers helped turn America into the apocalyptic Orwellian hell it is today, died recently after his body crashed and lost all paper records of his T-cells.

Diebold first became interested in automation in the Navy during World War II when he observed a ship's mechanized antiaircraft controls blowing up ballots.

In 1961 he and his firm, the Diebold Group, designed the first electronic network able to link bank account records and then route the information directly to Satan.

Diebold is survived by his wife, two daughters, and millions of disenfranchised voters.

Jim Earl

Maurice Graham, King of the Hobos

King of the Hobos, Maurice Graham, finally caught the Westbound Train last week, after telling loved ones he was doggin' it to a couple of soup bowls for a handful of snipes and some spear biscuits. At first, witnesses thought he was just chucking a dummy in order to give a bull and a couple of bone polishers the slip. While others thought maybe he caught a bug after frying up some bad micks on his banjo.

Even the local punks said maybe he'd gone rum-dum for the corner slop-tart. But they were easy marks and soon were back honey-dipping at the county big house. Suffice it to say, Maurice is up in heaven packin' the mustard, hittin' the grit, sharin' some nickel notes, and jawbonin' around the boodle. Yep, all's hunky-dory in clown town.

Mourning Remembrance

I have no friggin' idea what all that means. But I do know this: There's one less guy in stinky clothing taking a dump in the Amtrak parking lot.

A perennial favorite, Graham was voted National Hobo King five times at Iowa's annual hobo convention after two other contestants were frozen out of the competition when they were discovered frozen out in the asparagus car.

Graham once told reporters, quote, "A hobo is just a guy who went camping and never came home." By the way, that description also applies to ax murderers.

When he finally returned home for good, the white-bearded Graham adopted a new identity by dressing up as Santa Claus and spending the next 30 years puzzling children by asking them for work.

Graham requested people throw down half a yard or at least an ace-spot or two to help fellow yeggs get unhooked from speed ballin' ink.

Jim Earl

Chet Helms, Father of San Francisco's Summer of Love

Chet Helms, father of San Francisco's 1967 Summer of Love and leader of that decade's hippie subculture, finally got "back to the land" this month when he was buried in it.

Authorities say the renowned promoter of hippie philosophy and psychedelic light-shows was found alone in his house, sprawled on the ceiling.

Among other things, Helms is famous for persuading Janis Joplin to move to San Francisco in 1962. The move was responsible for changing the face of music forever as well as precipitating the "Great San Francisco Heroin Shortage of 1963."

Doctors said the cause of death was attributed to repetitive stress injuries directly related to, quote, "Years of helping kids fly their freak-flags."

Mourning Remembrance

Steve Jobs, "Dear Leader"

Steve Jobs, the computer pioneer who co-founded Apple and inspired people all over the world to "think outside the box," is now stuck inside one.

Sources say just moments before his death, the ailing Jobs turned beige and dragged himself into the trash for deletion.

The news came as a shock to countless Apple fans, who still insist they're not going to buy his death until a later version comes out.

Historians rate Jobs on a par with Thomas Edison. Mainly because they both loved to make silent movies of guys with big mustaches sneezing.

Jim Earl

A true visionary, he was the first to see the real commercial potential of the graphical user-interface. Especially when it was made in Chinese sweat shops.

Among his many patents was the "Hockey-puck shaped mouse," or as Chinese workers call it, "the only thing strong enough to snap my neck after securing the chord to an eighth floor railing so that I may leave this daily torture and finally taste the sweet relief that is death - mouse."

Jobs recently fought hard for city planners to approve his new company headquarters built in the style of a spaceship. The hope was to attract non-union labor from Pluto who only eat discarded Zunes.

Jobs' last wish was for Apple Police to search the surrounding neighborhood in order to find out which one of his employees accidentally took home his liver.

This obit was made on a Mac.

Mourning Remembrance

Paul K. Keene, Organic Farming Pioneer

Paul K. Keene, the former mathematics professor, avowed pacifist, and organic farmer who, "just wanted to go back to the land," got his wish this week when he was buried in it.

In the late 1930s while teaching in northern India, Keene met Mohandas Gandhi, whose belief in simple living inspired Keene to get the hell out of India and start a multimillion-dollar business.

For more than 50 years, Keene's Walnut Acres Farm produced a wide selection of products including peanut butter, granola, and instruction booklets on how to sit cross-legged on the lawn wearing Earth Shoes while playing a flute and deflecting rocks thrown by the "cool kids."

In the 1940s and 50s Keene's views on organic farming were considered eccentric. So much so, that some people labeled him a communist and even burned crosses on his lawn, incidents that probably led to his debut of the world's first organic urine-based fire extinguisher.

Keene requested his remains be buried with "sea salt and love."

Jim Earl

Jef Raskin, Macintosh Computer Pioneer

Jef Raskin, the software developer behind Apple Computer's pioneering "graphical user interface," died this month when he inexplicably froze up after making a series of cute frog noises.

A coroner's examination later revealed his system was full of bugs.

Legend has it that Raskin named the Macintosh computer after his favorite kind of apple. Other potential names included the "Bramley Pippin," "Luxton's Cornish Tart," and the poorly received "Tyderman's Mealy-Yellow Varietal."

Raskin's latest project featured a computer interface designed to operate on any operating system, including Windows and Apple. And for that reason alone, Bill Gates and Steve Jobs had to have him killed.

Raskin requested his body be packed up using his own box and shipped to the Apple Recycling Center.

Mourning Remembrance

Paul Sawyer, NASCAR Pioneer

Paul Sawyer, beloved pioneer of NASCAR racing, died this month after realizing he dedicated most of his adult life to the most boring sport on earth.

A true visionary, Sawyer helped develop stock car racing from a small town sport into one of the scariest incarnations of conservative southern thinking since Quantrill's Raiders slaughtered 400 abolitionists in 1863.

It all began in 1955 when Sawyer bought three small dirt tracks in Virginia and North Carolina, and turned them into state-of-the-art 100,000-seat racing arenas - all kept spotlessly clean by Strom Thurmond's illegitimate black kids.

Sawyer requested his body be cremated after being hurled at 200 miles per hour into a concrete retaining wall.

Jim Earl

Ed Schantz, Botox Pioneer

Ed Schantz, the military researcher who first purified the nerve poison used in Botox injections, was declared dead April 27. Schantz really died two years ago, but family members had a hard time telling the difference between his usual frozen expression and death.

In the 1960s, Schantz discovered that small doses of the botulinum toxin could help stop certain medical conditions, like aging gracefully.

Today, botulinum toxin injections are used to smooth out wrinkles and ultimately distract attention away from the fact that Joan Rivers has never been funny.

One of Botox's first medical uses was to treat crossed eyes, a condition usually caused by trying to visualize what Carrot Top's face used to look like.

The Pentagon requested Schantz's body be isolated in a hermetically sealed container so its toxins can be studied for possible use on the battlefield.

Mourning Remembrance

Jim Earl

Politics

Mourning Remembrance

General Sani Abacha, Nigerian Dictator

General Sani Abacha, one of Nigeria's most notorious and reclusive dictators, became even more reclusive yesterday when his lifeless body was whisked off to an unmarked grave.

Abacha, who had close ties to the right-wing Christian group "The Family," died after he was allegedly poisoned by six teenage Indian prostitutes imported from Dubai, or as Senator John Ensign called it, "natural causes."

Political opponents hailed Abacha's death as the most progressive move of his career.

Nigerians are hopeful his sudden death will bring an end to the latest in a long string of military dictatorships and usher in a long-awaited string of "civilian" dictatorships.

Recently Abacha had made few public appearances, fueling speculation he was cutting a double album.

Near the end, Abacha defended his misuse of $4 billion dollars in oil revenue from the impoverished country by claiming he sank most of it in a string of Kenny Rogers roasted chicken outlets.

Abacha asked that mourners provide a bank account where his remains can be transferred, after which they will receive 15 percent of his body as compensation for their effort. My two children died in a car accident one month ago, and I have a blood clot in my leg. Please, I beg you in the name of God to help me collect this $10 million and the interest accrued on the direct deposit from Allied Bank PLC.

Thank you and God Bless - Mr. Wumi Abdul

Jim Earl

Lou Carrol, the Man Who Gave Nixon the Dog Checkers

Lou Carrol, the man who gave Richard Nixon the cocker spaniel that saved his career, is dead after suffering through 54 years of being known as the man who gave Richard Nixon the cocker spaniel that saved his career.

Doctors at the scene pronounced Carrol, "Dead, Now More Than Ever."

One summer day in 1952, Carrol packed the puppy into a crate addressed to the Nixon daughters, an act that destined the poor dog to suffer a lifetime of false recrimination every time their dad farted.

The cocker spaniel was to become Nixon's most famous political asset alongside his steely eyed glare, clammy handshake and uncanny ability to lie about almost everything.

That act has been credited with altering the course of American history, as well as giving dogs everywhere another reason to piss in their master's slippers.

Carrol is survived by a wife, two sons, and the looming punishment of being hounded for an eternity in hell by the embittered ghost of a vengeful cocker spaniel.

Mourning Remembrance

Michael Evans, Ronald Reagan's Photographer

Michael Evans, a photojournalist responsible for some of the most beloved photographs of Ronald Reagan, died at his home this week after his heart "just said no" to life.

Evans was Reagan's personal photographer from 1975 through 1985, having taken over the duties from Reagan's previous photographers starting with Thomas Edison.

Evans' 1975 close-up photo of Reagan smiling and wearing a cowboy hat became a symbol of the "great communicator" who once declared catsup a vegetable, told poor people he hoped they get botulism, and said trees cause more smog than cars.

Evans once told NPR, "What you saw with Ronald Reagan was what you got," adding, "which is why I knew he had to be stopped."

Mr. Evans is survived by two daughters, a son, and countless negatives of Reagan forgetting how to put on his trousers.

Jim Earl

Michael S. Joyce, Conservative

Michael Joyce, president of the Bradley Foundation and a leader in the rise of neoconservatism during the 1990s, is now compassionately dead.

In the 1990s his movement threw thousands of Wisconsin residents off welfare rolls, forcing them to sleep in parks where they huddled together for warmth in their giant, novelty "Cheesehead" hats.

In 2001 with the encouragement of Karl Rove, Joyce created "Americans for Community and Faith-Centered Enterprise." This led to other successful spin-off organizations like "Christian First, Jew Last," "Eat the Poor," and "That Sore on Your Penis Is Because You're Black."

Over the years Joyce's foundation has given away over $280 million in the fight to allow vouchers for religious schools, an effort that has kept thousands of innocent children from ever having to undergo the trauma of reading the Constitution.

Joyce requested his body be laid out on a dining room table and fondled by local Teamsters. Because, let's face it, everybody's got their kinky side.

Joyce also requested his remains be dried, pressed into anti-abortion leaflets, and passed out at local kindergartens.

Mourning Remembrance

Edward von Kloberg III, PR Man to the Dictators

Edward Joseph von Kloberg III, representative to such monstrous tyrants as Saddam Hussein and Nicolae Ceaucescu of Romania, committed suicide last week after losing his highest-paying client, President Bush.

A legend in Washington's public relations circles, Kloberg's clients included some of the late 20th century's most corrupt and murderous governments and public figures. Still, he was a good dancer.

Early in his career, Kloberg added "van" to his surname. Later he changed it to "von" to make it sound more distinguished, and later still, changed it to Cougar Mellencamp when he thought it might sell more of his crappy rock ballads.

Kloberg apparently leaped to his death from a castle in Rome. A master of spin until the end, Kloberg left a long suicide note explaining how he was, quote, "Just going out to consult with some of my former clients in hell."

Jim Earl

Helen Murphy, White House Gift Shop Manager

Helen Murphy, who for over a generation managed the gift shop in the East Wing of the White house, has died of frustration after failing to unload 12 crates of William Howard Taft scented candles.

While Murphy recalled how thrilling it was to meet every American leader from Richard M. Nixon through Bill Clinton, she was perhaps most impressed after running into President Nancy Reagan.

Retiring from the gift shop before the 2000 election, Murphy regretted never seeing any of the newer products, like the George W. Bush Snow Globe, full of actual cocaine powder, the Bill of Rights Doormat and the Lynne Cheney "My Daughter's Not a Lesbian" Flannel Shirt and Mullet Wig.

Friends say during slow days at the shop, Murphy would often enjoy reading, solving crossword puzzles, and watching Richard Nixon carry on drunken conversations with the Lincoln poster.

Murphy requested her body be stamped with the Presidential Seal and made into a tote bag.

Mourning Remembrance

Paul K. Perry, Political Statistician

Political statistician, Paul K. Perry, is now a dead issue.

Witnesses say this pioneer in the field of political polling reportedly dropped dead of a stroke after he was asked, "When did you stop beating your wife?"

Working with George Gallup from the beginning of modern public opinion surveys in the 1930s, Perry played a critical role in telling the public how they felt when they really didn't feel that way.

Perry is credited with at least two innovations.
One: devising a system to identify likely voters, and
Two: calling them up just when they're about to have dinner.

According to a recent poll, 30% of Perry's doctors said he'd probably die before last week, 38% said it would happen this week, and 75% said they still think Dewey beat Truman.

Jim Earl

J.B. Stoner, White Supremacist

J.B. Stoner, a proud racist-anti-Semite implicated in at least 12 bombings of black churches during the 1960s, is dead after his heart exploded under suspicious circumstances.

A prime suspect in the 1958 bombing of a Baptist Church in Alabama, Stoner wasn't indicted until 1977. Which is understandable. I mean, that paperwork has got to be a bitch. And folks are so much more laid back down there, right?

A real go-getter, Stoner at age 18 revived a dormant chapter of the KKK in Tennessee. A few years later he headed the "Stoner Christian Anti-Jewish Party." And a few years after that, he headed the "Stop Making Drug Jokes About My Last Name and Pay Attention to What I'm Doing" Anti-Catholic Society.

When his trial finally took place, the jury found him guilty in 90 minutes, one-forth the time it took him to write the note he tossed through the church window reading, "Me make black church box go boom now."

In 1974, the popular racist ran for lieutenant governor of Georgia, drawing nearly 10 percent of that state's crucial "crazy sons of bitches" vote.

Stoner requested his body never apologize for anything - even if it's brought back to life in the future by black scientists in a Jewish hospital.

Mourning Remembrance

Caspar Weinberger, Reagan's Secretary of Defense

Caspar Weinberger, the man who served as the evil teat of inspiration for three Republican presidents and oversaw the most expensive buildup of the military in peacetime history, is now Caspar the Friendly Ghost.

Doctors say Weinberger died of pneumonia, apparently the result of spending too many years leading the Cold War.

While director of the budget under Nixon, Weinberger earned the nickname "Cap the Knife," not because he cut the education budget, but because he used to masturbate into his cap while listening to recordings of Bobby Darin.

Jim Earl

But it was while Weinberger served as defense secretary for Ronald Reagan in 1981 that he really made his most important contribution: national debt.

Under Reagan, Weinberger was a crucial proponent of the missile-based Strategic Defense Initiative, Star Wars, or as Reagan later called it, "Who am I?"

Weinberger requested he be laid to rest in a coffin put together with common metal bolts that cost 80 cents in 1980, but had somehow become worth $39.00 two years later.

Mourning Remembrance

Jim Earl

Religion

Mourning Remembrance

Owen Allred, Polygamous Leader

Owen Allred, head of one of Utah's largest polygamous denominations, has died from complications of nagging. He was 91 and apparently thrived on aggravation.

Over his lifetime he had 8 wives, raised 48 children, and was estimated to have possessed the country's largest collection of "World's Best Dad Who Sleeps With 8 Other Women" mugs.

Owen's death was announced by his son Owen Jr., his son Owen Jr., his other son Owen Jr., and of course, his son Owen Jr.

In a *New York Times* interview three years ago, Allred said, quote, "People have the wrong idea that we're old-time kooks who prey on young girls," he added, "I also like my meat well-seasoned, if you know what I mean. You're not gonna print that, are you?"

Allred leaves behind two hundred grandchildren and four households full of laundry.

Jim Earl

Susan Atkins, Born Again Christian

Susan Atkins, whose fame stems mainly from the fact that she's not nearly as cute as Squeaky Fromme, is dead

Atkins lived a quiet, middle-class existence during her early years, singing in her church choir and helping out with numerous charity stabbings.

After running away from home, the teenage Atkins was fortunate enough to meet up with our lord and savior, Jesus Christ, who asked her to live with him at Spahn's Ranch.

It was there that Jesus taught her the finer points of robbery, murder, and pitching songs to music executives.

Atkins bragged that at the crime scene she tasted the blood of Sharon Tate. But what she didn't know was that Tex Watson secretly replaced the blood of Tate with that of coffee heiress Abigail Folger. Let's see how she reacts!

Relatives and loved-ones can console themselves with the thought that Susan is now up in heaven giving gonorrhea to Dennis Wilson.

Jim Earl

Rosemary Kooiman, Pagan Witch

Rosemary Kooiman, a pagan witch who won the legal right to perform pagan weddings in Virginia, died this month of a heart attack apparently while pleasuring herself with a broom and a five-pointed star.

In the 1960s Kooiman got a job at NASA testing space suits. And at one point she was in charge of shaking them out for moon dust. But friends say her most interesting NASA job was casting evil spells on two space shuttle missions.

Kooiman first rejected Christianity in the 1970s when it became obvious that a benevolent all-seeing God never would have allowed Disco.

She later compiled a three-year study course on her neopagan beliefs in response to her friends frequent questions like, "Why did you strangle my cat?" And, "Seriously. Why'd you strangle my cat?"

Kooiman requested her body be laid to rest near the guy who played the first Darrin Stephens.

Mourning Remembrance

Osama bin-Laden, Billionaire Industrialist, Businessman, Entrepreneur, Religious Icon & Chick Magnet

Osama bin-Laden, the shy yet dedicated business major who turned his father's construction business into a worldwide concern, is dead at the age of 52 after guiding his head and chest areas at a speed of 600 miles an hour into two American bullets.

Growing up in a large family, Osama never forgot the shame of having to be the 17th in line to use his brothers' hand-me-down ankle porn.

After his father died, Osama quickly immersed himself in all aspects of the construction industry. But it wasn't until the mid-1990s that he branched out into demolition.

Jim Earl

The end finally came when Navy Seals found him hiding out between the two old vaudeville towns of Abbot-abad & Costello-abad.

Mr. Laden was officially declared dead on May 2nd, which is kinda strange because his Facebook page is still sending me invites to suicide bombings. What if there's a conflict with one of Dane Cook's events?

The White House still insists President Obama refused to release bin-Laden's death pictures for security reasons, and not because they were lost at the local Foto-Abottabad Mat.

According to the White House web site, there's absolutely no way the public can see bin-Laden's death photos unless they upgrade to a premium subscription and download their assassination app.

Speaking of mass murderers, can we finally dig up Ray Kroc and shoot him too?

Among the many items found in the compound were details of bin-Laden's insidious new plot to make it so we, "just can't have nice things anymore."

Navy Seals also found bin-Laden's personal journal. Here are a few experts:

Compound Diary

9am
Dear Compound Diary, last night I dreamed I was eating a giant ball of cotton candy, and when I woke up my beard was gone.

Mourning Remembrance

10am
Busy day today. Everyone's running around like contractors with their heads cut off.

11am
I gotta get more exercise. Mustn't let the guys see me get Fatwa.

2pm
Today wife #3 complained about being cooped up here and demanded I take her someplace she's never been before. So I showed her the kitchen. Then I cut her head off.

3pm
What's the deal with socks? How come there's no "left" sock or "right" sock? There's just… "socks!"

4pm
At first I had my doubts about this neighborhood, but I think this place is really gonna work out juuuust fine.

In the end, I suppose everyone will have their own story about where they were when they first heard the news that Osama bin-Laden's death changed nothing.

The deceased requested his body be buried at sea and washed up on the lagoon so Gilligan can accidentally bring him back to life.

Jim Earl

Anton LaVey, Spiritual Leader

Anton LaVey, founder of the Church of Satan, is dead of heart failure, the result of years of trying to compete with the Republican Party.

LaVey was a man of many interests, always drawn to the unexplored and unexplained. For example: close associates say the High Priest of Evil once spent three years trying to figure out how Fig Newtons were made.

By the early 1970s, his church began to splinter, with many of its members going over to the Southern Baptists and even more into show business.

Mourning Remembrance

Ever the prolific creator, LaVey wrote five books during his career including, *The Satanic Bible* and the helpful *Men Are From Mars and Women Are From Hell*.

After suffering heart failure in 1990, LaVey rarely left his home except to shop at bulk discount stores for "sinfully" low-priced boxes of Depends.

His 100-year-old family home is appointed throughout with red ceilings, black walls, pentagrams, daggers, skulls, and the complete collection of Jim Varney videos.

LaVey eventually became known as "the black pope," "Satan's minion," and "that idiot in the black cape who ruined a perfectly good Victorian home."

For years he kept a lion and a tarantula as pets, and could often be seen around the neighborhood picking up "wicked" lumps of lion and tarantula poop using nothing more than a plastic baggy covering his hands.

His final book, *Satan Speaks*, scheduled for posthumous release, will focus on the proper way to trap yourself in a lifelong joke no one will ever get.

Jim Earl

Henry Morris, Father of Modern Creationism

Henry Morris, a hydraulics engineer who became known as the father of modern creationism and intelligent design, is dead after a series of divinely created strokes naturally selected his heart for failure.

Morris was born in Dallas, Texas, where people are so bone-jarringly stupid, it's not surprising how someone might believe God created them all as part of some cruel, party dare with Satan.

In his attempts to scientifically explain the theory of divine creation, Morris wrote more than 60 books, all of them starting with the sentence, "Hey, I know this is gonna sound hilarious, but hear me out on this. And I am NOT drunk."

In his landmark book, *The Genesis Flood*, Morris calculated the capacity of Noah's ark at roughly 522 railroad cars. Enough to hold 35,000 animals and over 100 smelly hobos.

Using the Bible as a factual account of history, Morris explained how the world could be created in six 24-hour days. His conclusion? On the first day, God created meth.

Since 1981, his Institute for Creation Research has awarded about 100 master's degrees, mostly to male loners in aluminum foil helmets who happen to live in their vans across the street from abortion clinics.

Morris is survived by thousands of embarrassed hydraulics engineers.

Mourning Remembrance

Adrian P. Rogers, Tool of God

Reverend Adrian P. Rogers, president of the ultra right-wing Southern Baptist Convention that helped usher in a resurgence of fundamentalist Christians in politics, died when his heart gave out after snorting eight-balls and performing oral sex on twelve men at the same time. Keep in mind, some of this information may be faulty.

Associates say Rogers' mesmerizing stage presence helped reinvigorate the fundamentalist Christian message that everything in the Bible should be taken literally. Except for all the embarrassingly stupid parts, which God meant for the Mormons.

He founded the Love Worth Finding ministry which broadcasts TV and radio programs worldwide to millions of people eagerly awaiting God's message that they're all worthless crap.

Rogers was so popular in Memphis, that church members would sometimes gather at the airport to greet his returning flights and then shrink in fear at the incredible metal bird that was never mentioned in the Bible.

Rogers is survived by 16 million Southern Baptists who still think Earth is 200 years old.

Jim Earl

Science

Mourning Remembrance

Alastair Cameron, Developed Giant Impact Theory

Alastair Cameron, the astrophysicist who first theorized the moon was formed billions of years ago after Earth collided with another planet, died recently when a chunk of arterial plaque collided with his heart.

His Giant Impact theory of 1976 was widely mocked until overshadowed by Elton John teaming up with Kiki Dee.

Cameron's "giant impact" theory postulated that the moon was created after an object the size of Mars struck Earth, leaving huge amounts of rubble in its wake that eventually formed the moon and parts of the Bronx.

In his quest for answers, Cameron also discovered how gigantic dying stars create new stars as they explode. In other words, he helped solve the mystery of Lisa Marie Presley's career.

Cameron requested his body be hurled at light speed into Paul Sorvino.

Jim Earl

Sidney Gottlieb, LSD Scientist

Sidney Gottlieb, the CIA chemist who secretly dosed hundreds of unsuspecting Americans with LSD in the name of national security, was found dead in his rural Virginia home, sprawled on the ceiling.

For almost two decades starting in the 1950s, the CIA gave hallucinogenic drugs to scores of innocent Americans because they feared enemies could use the drugs as a weapon, or even worse, to get "far out."

Many of the victims suffered permanent psychological damage. In a particularly tragic case, one even went on to play bass for the Beach Boys.

Shortly before retiring in 1972, a regretful Gottlieb conceded that his experiments had been useless but fun to watch.

After leaving the CIA, Gottlieb and his wife performed humanitarian work. They even ran a leprosy hospital in India for about 18 months until they discovered they were just tripping in their hotel room.

Gottlieb requested his body be cut into tiny squares and sold at People's Park in Berkeley.

Jim Earl

Horace Hagedorn, Fertilizer Giant

Horace Hagedorn, beloved founder of Miracle-Gro plant food, became his own compost last week at the age of 89.

A source close to the family said Hagedorn passed mysteriously in the middle of the night, surrounded by millions of dead sardines.

Over the years, loyalty and recognition for the Miracle-Gro brand grew to such heights, that in the 1960s Hagedorn was inspired to come up with the motto, "Miracle-Gro doesn't have customers, it has fans." This was quickly followed up with the mottos, "Miracle-Gro is bigger than Jesus" and "I am the lizard king. Who's gonna come up here and love my ass?"

Through his leadership, Mr. Hagedorn built Miracle-Gro into a giant chemical conglomerate, and also one of the world's foremost sources of deformed testicles and children born without eyes.

Today, Mr. Hagedorn's popular blue fertilizer is used by millions of gardeners around the world, along with an ever-growing number of Idaho militias and paramilitary groups.

Hagedorn requested his ashes be applied in a two-inch layer beneath a tulip bulb.

Jim Earl

George Lenchner, Prominent Mathematician

George Lenchner, a popular math educator who championed national interscholastic math leagues, is dead of "severe wedgie complications."

Lenchner was executive director of Math Olympiads for Elementary and Middle Schools, a nonprofit organization he founded to help kids deal with the trauma of getting shoved into their lockers.

A gifted pianist, a youthful Lenchner once toured in the Borscht Belt with Moe Howard who taught him the maximum number of times an audience could laugh at, "Moe, Larry the cheese!" before asking for a refund.

Mr. Lenchner is survived by his two sons: one running at 10 miles per hour from a bully in Chicago, and the other running at 7 miles per hour from a bully in New York. If each bully is traveling 2 miles an hour faster than each of the sons, then how long before someone gets their glasses broken?

The deceased asked that he be buried in his pocket protector.

Mourning Remembrance

John DeLorean, Famed Chemist

John DeLorean, former vice president of General Motors and creator of the self-named sports car of the 1980s, died in New Jersey when his pump gave out after nearly 25 years of running away from creditors.

In 1964 as a General Motors designer, he created his first "muscle car" by cramming a V-8 engine into a Pontiac and calling it the GTO. Twenty years later as head of DeLorean Motors, he created his first arrest by cramming 220 pounds of cocaine into a suitcase and calling it "police entrapment."

DeLorean's construction technique was considered by many to be revolutionary. Not because he made cars out of space-age materials with gull-wing doors, but because he was dumb

Jim Earl

enough to build them in Belfast. I mean, who the hell wants a car made in Belfast?

The deceased requested his memorial service feature a coffin with a lid that opens upward and outward for easy, unobstructed viewing access.

Mourning Remembrance

Jacob Marinsky, Discovered Promethium

Jacob Marinsky, the first human to isolate the radioactive element promethium, died last month well past his half-life.

Marinsky named the radioactive element after the Greek god Prometheus, who stole fire from heaven for humanity and then gave everyone cancer.

Number 61 on the Periodic Table, Promethium is a man-made soft beta emitter existing in two allotropic forms. A non-gamma ray discharger, promethium's particles can impinge on elements of high atomic numbers and even generate X-rays. Wheew. Is it just me, or are you getting horny?

In 1990, the University at Buffalo awarded Marinsky the Clifford Furnas Memorial Award in honor of graduates willing to continue living in Buffalo.

Even though he was a passionate supporter of the civil rights movement and an early opponent of the Vietnam War, most people still remember him as that guy who made the eyes glow on all those Kit-Cat clocks.

Marinsky requested his body be washed in a solution of salt resins, bombarded with neurons, and then used as an auxiliary power source for space probes.

Jim Earl

Maynard J. Ramsay, Renowned Buggerer

Maynard J. Ramsay, an internationally recognized expert on exotic insects, died last month after he got trapped between the window pane and the screen.

Every weekday for over 30 years, Dr. Ramsay commuted from his home on Staten Island to his Agriculture Department job in Manhattan simply by burrowing into a piece of rotted melon and washing up on the banks of the Hudson.

Ramsay was a former president of the Insecticide Society of Washington, which eventually had to be renamed the *Cancer Society of Washington*.

Ramsay was perhaps best known for his work on the potato parasite. Not for his groundbreaking research, but because that's all he'd talk about on dates. Potato bugs. And that kind of stuff really gets around, you know? I mean, what a buzz-kill.

Sources say that for the last few years of his life, Ramsey survived on nothing but crumbs. His funeral was a catered affair, and according to witnesses, it was attended by many ants.

The deceased requested his body be impaled on a No. 5 pin, allowed to dry, and then mounted on a piece of cardboard for viewing.

Mourning Remembrance

Show Business

Jim Earl

Mourning Remembrance

Lew Anderson, Clarabell the Clown on *Howdy Doody*

Lew Anderson, whose iconic portrayal of Howdy Doody's mischievous Clarabell influenced future clown Courtney Love, is now jammin' up in Heaven with John Wayne Gacy.

Anderson's popular character, Clarabell, became famous for communicating with others using horn toots and water squirts - two things Anderson started doing again when he turned 80.

Many believe Anderson's portrayal of Clarabell as a mute was a stroke of comedic genius. Or just the producer's little way of never having to pay scale.

A distinctive feature of the hit show were the on-stage bleachers of 40 kids called the "Peanut Gallery," so-named because "Fear-Poop Arcade" just didn't seem appropriate.

Jim Earl

Anderson requested he also be remembered for a lifetime spent working as a respected and accomplished jazz musician. Buuut I don't think that's gonna happen.

Mourning Remembrance

Henry Corden, Voice of Fred Flintstone

Henry Corden, who for almost 30 years was famous for voicing the character of Fred Flintstone with his iconic "Yabba-dabba-doo!" is now "Yabba-dabba-dead."

Corden reportedly died of multiple puncture wounds after trying to use a porcupine as a hairbrush and shave himself with a clamshell full of bumblebees.

Besides the popular cartoon series, Corden also supplied his voice for a string of specials such as "The Flintstones New Neighbors," "Fred's Final Fling," and "Fred and Barney Get Gonorrheastone."

Corden requested his remains be interned inside the beak of a priceless Pterodactyl skeleton.

Jim Earl

Gerard Damiano, Director of the Film *Deep Throat*

Gerard Damiano, director of the film *Deep Throat*, is now deep-sixed.

Word of his death came as a shock to loved ones, who found the news hard to swallow. You could say they were all choked up.

The director suffered a stroke in September, 34 years after Linda Lovelace suffered hundreds of strokes - in her windpipe.

Friends recalled how on a typical shoot, the playful director loved gags. Off the set, he was known to take life by the balls and jam it into your mouth.

Mourning Remembrance

Released in 1972, *Deep Throat* was the first porn picture to be shown in cinemas since *Ben-Hur*.

The film created a sensation and was followed up with *Deep Butt* and the poorly received *Deep Hand*.

Though Damiano made numerous porn films, *Deep Throat* was always his "bread and man-butter."

The movie gave Linda Lovelace her first speaking role with the immortal line, "Glub glub."

Damiano began his porn career in the late 1960s at the suggestion of his accountant who said there'd never be a better time to take advantage of low dry-cleaning rates.

Damiano requested his remains be swallowed without any bullshit whining from you.

Jim Earl

Bob Denver, Actor. Roll Model. Gilligan.

Bob Denver, whose hilarious incompetence kept the castaways from ever escaping Gilligan's Island, finally escaped from life this month when his doctor was unable to patch a defective heart valve using only coconuts and spare radio parts.

Denver graduated from Loyola University in the 1950s with a bachelor's in political science, a degree he later put to good use by making America even more stupid than it was before.

Shortly after Denver's passing, the California State Senate agreed unanimously to adjourn in Denver's memory. And in his honor, they agreed to bungle every opportunity to escape from the reign of Arnold Schwarzenegger.

Mourning Remembrance

Though deep in grief, Denver's fans can console themselves with the thought that he's now up in heaven getting creeped out by Bob Crane.

When reached for comment, Russell Johnson said he should have fucked Mary Ann while he had the chance.

Denver is survived by (sung to the *Gilligan's Island* theme) "his granddaughter, and his wife. His son Patrick, and the rest, gathered at Forrest Lawn."

Jim Earl

Lillian Bounds Disney, Wife of Walt

Lillian Bounds Disney, wife of cartoon mogul Walt Disney, died peacefully in her sleep Tuesday accompanied by funny sound effects and exploding asterisks above her head.

For 41 years, Lillian Disney worked patiently in the background, raising their family and serving as a sounding board for her husband's scary reactionary beliefs and weird hand-washing rituals.

She first met Walt Disney in 1917 and was instantly charmed by his brash dreams of achieving fame and fortune by stealing the ideas of others.

Lillian was credited with advising Walt to rename the now legendary mouse character "Mickey" instead of the original "Mortimer." She also persuaded Walt to abandon another new character entirely, the ill-conceived "Heinrich The Storm Trooping Hedgehog."

For years after her husband's death, the devoted Lillian said she could always feel the reassuring presence of Walt watching over her - from within a liquid nitrogen tank suspended above her bed.

The deceased requested her body be taller than the bottom of the sign in order to ride on the "20,000 Leagues Under the Cemetery" ride.

James Dougherty, Marilyn Monroe's First Husband

James Dougherty, an ex-cop who's main claim to fame was being the first of three men to be divorced by Marilyn Monroe, died this month, mercifully just in time to avoid hearing another crappy tribute song by Elton John.

After they got married in 1942, he and Marilyn moved into a tiny studio apartment with a pull-down Murphy bed. It was here where Dougherty would often, "pull down her Murphy."

During his second marriage, Dougherty once appeared on *To Tell the Truth* as Marilyn's first husband. When she found out, his second wife threw a pan at him. This led him to destroy hundreds of letters from Monroe reportedly worth a fortune. When she found out, his second wife threw another pan at him.

In 1986 he ran for Congressional office, but lost when the people of his state said they wanted a divorce in order to pursue an acting career.

Family members say they can console themselves with the thought that Dougherty's up in Heaven, getting the crap beat out of him by Joe DiMaggio.

Jim Earl

Len Dresslar, Voice of The Jolly Green Giant

Len Dresslar, whose booming rendition of the Jolly Green Giant's "Ho Ho Ho" inspired a whole generation of children to flee in fear at the sight of spinach, died last week in a "ho, ho, hospital."

If Dressler's voice was familiar to millions of TV viewers for over 40 years, so too was the image of a huge, green-skinned monster straddling the valley of an innocent community, with its terrified farmers gazing up in disgust at the perverse sight of that droopy asparagus spear and two gigantic, wrinkled peas dangling high from within a loosely fitted toga.

Dresslar also played "Snap" in the Snap-Crackle-Pop Rice Krispies trio until he started letting Yoko Ono hang out with him during the recording sessions.

He was also the voice of the Marlboro Man, the guy who sang, "When you're out of Schlitz, you're out of beer," and after those gigs fell through, the guy you'd occasionally hear at your local bar yelling, "Who the hell you gotta blow ta get a cigarette and a beer in this dump? Huuuuh? You know who I AM? Ho hoo hooo –eyyacckk!"

Later in life, Dresslar often joked that thanks to the residuals from his "ho, ho, ho," his daughters didn't have to become "ho, ho ho's."

Dresslar requested that at the fleeting moment of perfect flavor, migrant farm workers cut off his Niblets, freeze them in a light butter sauce, and then vacuum pack them in flavor-tight pouches to retain their nutrients.

Mourning Remembrance

Ralph Edwards, TV Pioneer

Ralph Edwards, the host and creator of *Truth or Consequences* and *This is Your Life*, two of the most popular shows in television history, has just created another hit, called *This is My Death*.

During the 1950s his shows were so popular, a town in New Mexico renamed itself "Truth or Consequences." Unfortunately the "truth" was that it was too close to a nuclear testing range, and the "consequences" were cancer.

Every installment of *This Is Your Life* started the same way. Edwards would surprise a hapless celebrity with the phrase "This is your life!" whereupon the celebrity would finally get the message his career was over.

Jim Earl

Remaining active throughout his 92 years, Edwards also created such well-known shows as, *The People's Court, Name That Tune, The People's Consequences, Name That Court, The People's Tune,* and *Truth Court Consequences Tune People's Name The*.

Edwards requested his remains be surprised by a guy with a camera and microphone and then wheeled into a room full of annoying relatives.

Mourning Remembrance

George Gerbner, Television Researcher

George Gerbner, a professor at the Annenberg School for Communications who pioneered research on the influence of television violence on viewers' perceptions of reality, has died. But he'll come back next season when we all find out it was just a dream.

The 86-year-old Gerbner reportedly died after his grandchildren thought they could wake him from a nap by lighting a stick of dynamite in his mouth.

After three decades of study, Gerbner concluded America's youth were learning to read by watching television commercials and developing a consumer mentality. Man, I don't feel fresh. You got any douche?

Gerbner requested his remains be subjected to 6 to 8 incidents of violence per hour, and if children are watching, 20 to 35 incidents per hour.

Jim Earl

Phil Harris, Captain on *Deadliest Catch*, and Advocate of the Inverted Food Pyramid

Phil Harris, captain of the Cornelia Marie, one of the crab-fishing boats on the fantasy series *Deadliest Catch*, is now riding a rogue wave to the "vast Dead Sea."

Witnesses say the hard-livin', high-caloric sea captain suffered a massive stroke in port while attempting to offload three tons of Philadelphia Cheese Steaks from his lower intestine.

The news came as a shock to viewers, but not to friends who knew his favorite meal was often cold coffee-grounds mixed with congealed bacon fat and Xanax.

Mourning Remembrance

The crusty sea-fairer rose through the ranks of fishermen quickly, and by the time he was 20 became one of the youngest captains ever to have a 70-year-old body.

Despite desperate pleading from family and friends, the cantankerous Harris never changed his diet. And when the coroner split open his stomach he found two half-digested sharks, a gallon of brake fluid, and a metal folding-chair. Remember, readers: "It Drains To The Sea."

Reportedly his addiction for stimulants became so bad, every time they would approach a Mexican tanker he'd order the crew to tie him to the mast

Riding high on his popularity in 2008, Harris developed a line of coffees called "Captain's Reserve" with blends named after fishing themes like "Midnight Sunrise Blend," "Starboard Dolphin Blend," and "I Haven't Seen a Real Woman in 8 Months So Excuse My Raging Boner Blend" and "Seriously, Get Out of My Way, I Have a Raging Hard-On And You're The Only Warm Thing in This Cabin, I Don't Care If You Are My Best Friend's Son Who Was Entrusted To Me For Training on the High Seas, Stop Looking at Me Like That, No One Has to Find Out, And What if They Did? Do They Know the Pain? The Lonely Months I Spend Out Here Hoping for The Gentle Touch of A Reassuring Hand? You Don't Have to Tell Me, I Know What the Others Are Saying Behind My Back, They're All Disloyal, I Tried to Run The Ship Properly By the Book, But They Fought Me At Every Turn, Scoffing at Me and Spreading Wild Rumors About Steaming in Circles and Then I Was to Blame For Lieutenant Maryk's Incompetence and Poor Seamanship, They Laughed at Me and Made Jokes, But I Proved Beyond the Shadow of A Doubt, and With Geometric Logic That It's Possible to Sew a Dog's Head Onto A Mackerel and Sell It To School Children - Blend."

Jim Earl

Harris, who once stated, "You're not a man 'til you've pulled a tooth out of your mouth with a pair of pliers," also stated, "You're not somebody's bitch until the crew pulls a cleat-knot out of your ass with a winch."

During filming of the 7th season of *Deadliest Catch*, he suffered a massive stroke and doctors had to place Harris in an induced coma. It was during this period that friends say he made the most sense.

In tribute to his memory, the show's production company ordered their writers to produce a special show this time about shit that actually happens.

Harris requested his remains be crammed inside a turkey, deep-fried in chicken fat, and pickled inside a giant mason jar of Red Bull.

Mourning Remembrance

Paul Henning, Television Producer

Paul Henning, the television writer and producer who created hits like, *The Beverly Hillbillies*, *Petticoat Junction* and *Green Acres*, has finally been cancelled.

Henning reportedly died of a massive stroke upon seeing for the first time an episode of *Petticoat Junction*.

Mr. Henning came up with the idea for *The Beverly Hillbillies* based on childhood memories of his days in the Ozarks, in a little town where apparently every family had a banker with a lesbian secretary.

Historians say the *Hillbillies* episodes that aired in the weeks after JFK's assassination are still the highest-rated half-hour shows ever, owing to millions of shocked Americans hoping

Jim Earl

they might see FBI agents rough up the Clampetts as payback to the South.

Henning requested his body be buried anywhere obsessed fans couldn't get close enough to spray-paint his tomb with the words "Cee-ment pond," "vittles" and "Bugtussle."

Well doggie!

Mourning Remembrance

Bob Kane, Not Bob Crane

Bob Kane, the man who invented *Batman* and ruined Adam West's career, died at the age of 83 after witnesses reported seeing a strange green and yellow gas rise from beneath his covers.

Doctors knew the end was near when Kane ran out of his Special Anti-Death Bat Spray.

When Kane first drew *Batman* in 1939, the crime-fighter lacked the inherent powers of Superman and had to rely instead on his strength, agility, and legions of gay followers.

Batman's alter ego was Bruce Wayne, a rich man who vowed vengeance on criminals because as a boy, he watched a robber gun down his parents while they were dressing up as bats.

Jim Earl

Even though he received stacks of fan mail every day, Kane was still puzzled why so many of them asked about Colonel Klink.

Kane asked that his remains be kept cool and dry, encased in Mylar, and stored in an unheated room.

Mourning Remembrance

Gordon Lee, Child Star in the *Little Rascals*

Gordon Lee, the chubby child actor who played Porky in the *Little Rascals* comedies, died this week, thankfully before Robert Blake had a chance to kill him.

Lee became famous for appearing in more than 40 of the *Our Gang* shorts that were later syndicated for decades on TV. And sources say he literally earned hundreds of dollars.

The *Little Rascals* series made history for being one of the first film series where the African-American kid was portrayed with other stereotypes equally as disturbing, like the "sweaty fat boy," the "deformed frog-voiced kid," and the "slutty blonde girl."

In many of their comedies, Porky and Buckwheat teamed up against the older boys like Alfalfa. Interesting note: just 20 years later, fate and a slug from a 45 teamed up against Alfalfa's stomach.

Among the films Lee appeared in were 1936's *The Awful Tooth*, 1937's *Bored of Education*, and 1938's *That Hobo Touched Me Again*.

Family members are consoling themselves with the thought that right now, Lee's up in heaven lending Alfalfa some money for hooch.

Lee, whose character originated the catchphrase, "O-tay!," requested his remains be "'T-mated."

Jim Earl

Sid Luft, Judy Garland's Third Husband

Sid Luft, former Hollywood producer and Judy Garland's third husband, is now over the rainbow and under 6 feet of dirt.

Luft is widely credited with being responsible for Garland's comeback in the 1950s, as well as being the only man to ever love her who wasn't gay.

Before the couple's marriage, Luft had a reputation as an alcoholic brawler who had broken four noses in various bar fights. No wait. That's Judy Garland.

When Luft first met Garland, the singer was addicted to drugs, beset with depression, and perhaps most disturbing of all, still accepting phone calls from Mickey Rooney.

Family members are consoling themselves with the thought that Sid's up in Heaven with David Guest's original eyebrows.

Vaughn Meader, JFK Mimic

Vaughn Meader, the mimic, who in 1962 achieved instant fame satirizing president Kennedy, passed away recently, his last words being, "chowda, chowda, chowda."

His comedy LP, *The First Family*, became the fastest-selling record of its time, winning the Grammy for album of the year in 1962 over such fierce competition as, *It's A Gas*, Mad Magazine's wry tribute to belching.

Meader's career was cut short by the assassination of John Fitzgerald Kennedy. To distance himself from the sad association, Meader began going by his birth name. Unfortunately, his birth name was John Fitzgerald Kennedy.

Always the magnet for bad luck, Meader's subsequent career imitating Lee Harvey Oswald only lasted two days.

Bereaved fans say Meader's up in heaven, jammin' with some guy who used to do impressions of Lincoln.

Jim Earl

Ted Peshak, Director of Educational-Films

Ted Peshak, whose educational shorts on dating and personal hygiene taught a generation of schoolchildren how to become the laughing stock of their neighborhood, died last week after getting run over by Mr. Bungle.

Peshak made countless films, including one geared towards school kids called, *How Billy Keeps Clean*, and another geared towards employees of Hughes Aircraft called, *How It's Impossible to Ever Get Clean, No Matter How Long You Wash and Wash and Wash Your Hands. Store Your Urine in Jars.*

Ted leaves behind his sons Gary and Skip, two men who grew up learning the hard way that your emotions can be your greatest enemy, and that pleasant, unemotional conversation can help with the digestion.

Mourning Remembrance

Thurl Ravenscroft, the Voice of Tony the Tiger

Thurl Ravenscroft, whose booming voice of Tony the Tiger helped condemn two generations of American children to a life of high fructose corn syrup and tragic obesity, is now buried in a... Grrrrrrrave!

After leaving the Air Force in 1947, he went to Hollywood to form a vocal quartet called the Mellomen that performed with Danny Kaye, who Laurence Olivier once said was "Ggggaaaaaaaaay!"

While in the service, he once transported the British leader Winston Churchill, who was later quoted as saying, "Responsibility is the price of... Grrrrrreeeatness!"

Friends recall how Kellogg's cereal requested in 1952 that he write something for their new character, Tony the Tiger. After thinking about it for a while, the World War II vet came up the words that would immortalize him in the world of advertising, "Human entrails."

A religious man, Ravenscroft began narrating annual presentations at the Crystal Cathedral, and was known for ending his show with the phrase, "Kellogs Frosted Flakes, they're Grrrreat! But not as great as the lord Jesus Chrrrrrist who died on the crrrrrross for your sins, dirty heathens."

Those who worked with him often called him "unpretentious." While those who lived next door to him often called him "loud" and called the police whenever he was having sex.

Kellogs suggested his body be enjoyed every morning with skim milk and sliced bananas.

Jim Earl

Celebrity Dwarf, John Rice

John Rice, a Florida millionaire who at 2 feet, 10 inches was one of the world's shortest twins, tragically plunged to his death this week when he fell off a footstool.

Over the last 25 years, Rice and his equally small brother Greg became millionaires doing infomercials and acting in film —you know, mostly shorts.

As news of Rice's death spread, flags all around the state were lowered to one-quarter staff.

The owner of the local Honda dealership described Rice as a devoted civic booster, meaning he could never get in a Civic without a boost.

Mourning Remembrance

Rice's brother asked that John be remembered as the indomitable optimist, "Who always saw every glass as less than half full."

Rice is survived by his brothers, Sneezy, Dopey, Grumpy, Happy and of course Greg.

Jim Earl

Nipsey Russell, Comedian

Nipsey Russell, the comedian whose improvised poems made him one of television's most popular game-show guests during the 1970s, died last week after failing to come up with a funny rhyme for, "Help nurse!"

For years, Russell delighted audiences with his funny poems. One of his more memorable four-line verses was:

The opposite of pro is con;
That fact is clearly seen;
If progress means move forward,
Then what does Congress mean?

This was followed by the less popular,

Why the hell am I always getting scale?
I appear on every fuckin' game show on fuckin' TV.
And I can't get more than scale?
What the fuck is up with that? Fuck you, whitey!!

Russell isn't known for his film roles. Although he did make a memorable appearance in the all-black musical, *The Wiz*. Memorable because everything else in the film sucked.

Family members can console themselves with the thought that Russell's now up in heaven, competing with Foster Brooks for Dean Martin's approval.

Mourning Remembrance

Theodore F. Shaker, Former CEO of Arbitron Ratings Company

Last week the life of Theodore F. Shaker was cancelled after it was determined not enough white males in the 25-to-54 year-old age group were watching him.

Before becoming head of Arbitron in 1971, Shaker worked for two decades in network television as CEO in charge of drowning kittens.

Arbitron was originally called the American Research Bureau. But Shaker changed the name after hearing that it might alienate minorities, namely the five people who watched *My Mother the Car*.

Shaker requested his remains be sent to a random household and a diary be kept on how well his body holds up after being exposed to 13 weeks of *That '70s Show*.

Jim Earl

Spoony Singh, Founder of Hollywood Wax Museum

Spoony Singh, the eccentric entrepreneur who established the world famous Hollywood wax museum, died of congestive heart failure this week after a piece of plaque shaped like Delta Burke lodged in his aorta.

Born in India, Singh recalled growing up in a town so small, the wax museum was just a display of used Q-Tips.

Singh started the museum in 1964, when a nation still mourning the loss of a young president, longed to see actors made out of wax.

Here's some fun facts about the museum:

Mourning Remembrance

Because the camera adds 10 pounds to an actor's build, the museum strives to get the proportions correct every time, right down to the Olson twins' shapely 83 pound physiques.

More than 10 feet of leather was used to recreate Russell Crow's gladiator uniform, while over 20 feet of parchment was needed to duplicate his bar tab.

The wax figure of Dracula had to be moved to the White House exhibit in order to discourage stray cats from sleeping inside Barbara Bush's vagina.

Singh requested family members painstakingly replicate his remains in wax so they can use his melted body parts to remove unsightly back hair.

Jim Earl

Peter Smithers, Model for James Bond

Sir Peter Smithers, a World War II British spy who inspired Ian Fleming's character James Bond, died at age 92 last month after he mistook his folding sniper rifle for a cane and fell onto a deadly metal hat.

Smithers died at his home in Switzerland, where he had retired in 1970 to get away from all those annoying "shaken, not stirred" jokes.

During the war, Smithers served in British Naval Intelligence under Commander Ian Fleming. It was there that Fleming first got the idea to increase Britain's budget for expensive spy gadgets by cutting down on toothbrushes.

After the war, Smithers served in the British Parliament until he had to resign in 1964 when he couldn't convince reporters he really didn't know any girls named "Pussy."

Smithers requested his remains be buried in an exploding attaché case.

Mourning Remembrance

Aaron Spelling, Artist

Aaron Spelling, a man who touched millions of Americans by tapping into their deepest, inner loathing and then paying B-actors to portray it on television, has finally been canceled.

Spelling reportedly died of a heart attack somewhere in his massive 123-room mansion after daring someone he could turn off all the lights.

Spelling, who once said the secret to his success was, "knowing just how much the average person loves to watch the insecurities and foibles of the wealthy," was just about to start his newest project, *Rich People Fart*.

Spelling helped produce an impressive variety of shows like *Dynasty*, *The Love Boat*, *Fantasy Island*, *Charlie's Angels*, *Melrose*

Jim Earl

Place, The Love Island, Charlie's Boat, Melrose Hills, Boat Island Love Hills Dynasty Angels, and the ill-fated *Manson's Ranch.*

Spelling requested he be buried next to his daughter's original nose.

Mourning Remembrance

Herbert L. Strock, B-Movie Director

Herbert Strock, a B-movie director responsible for such creature features as, *I Was a Teenage Frankenstein*, *How to Make a Monster*, and *The Crawling Hand*, has died after years of not being able to live up to the genius of his early work.

Strock's 1979 masterpiece *The Monster* was also titled *Monstroid*, *The Toxic Monster*, *Monster, the Legend That Became a Terror*, and when those failed, *Deep Throat*.

But he is perhaps best remembered for his 1954 film *Gog* in which two robots in charge of a secret underground space lab go mad and attempt to stand up to the House Un-American Activities Committee.

Strock's finely crafted films helped launch the acting careers of such greats as Kent Taylor, Gail Ganley, Craig Duncan, and of course, Whit Bissel.

Strock requested his remains be distributed country-wide for less than a week at failing drive-ins, and then mocked for 45 years on late-night TV.

Jim Earl

Lennie Weinrib, Voice of *H.R. Pufnstuf*

Lennie Weinrib, who for 3 years helped write and voice the beloved children's fantasy show *H.R. Pufnstuf* set on Living Island, is now on Dead Island.

Weinrib reportedly died of a stroke when his overstuffed nerf refrigerator and the talking grandfather clock played keep-away with his heart medicine.

Although he had a long and exciting career in TV and movies, Wcinrib said nothing would ever equal the thrill of the first time he accidentally sat on Freddy the Flute.

Weinrib also did the voices for other Sid and Marty Krofft productions like *Magic Mongo*, *Sigmund and the Sea Monsters*, *Dr. Shrinker*, *Lidsville*, and the groundbreaking, *We've Run Out of Veiled Drug References Ville*.

Weinrib requested his head be expanded to outlandishly hideous proportions and his dead body be animated from the inside by midgets.

Mourning Remembrance

Thelma White, Actress

Thelma White, whose portrayal of a hard-boiled marijuana addict in the 1936 movie *Reefer Madness* inspired a whole generation of pot heads to laugh at getting far out, got further out than she ever could have imagined this month, when she died at the age of 94.

Born in 1910, White was the daughter of carnival performers who traveled throughout the Midwest entertaining children with low-budget exploitation skits about addiction to spirits of ipecac.

During her later years she went on to become an agent for actor Robert Blake, prompting the question: Where was she the night of the murder?

Relatives say the aged icon of weed was found dead in her living room - sprawled on the ceiling.*

Yes, that's the same joke I used for Sidney Gottlieb. Shut up.

Jim Earl

Robert Young, Actor

Robert Young, loved by millions of viewers as television's "unflappable, good-natured manic depressive father with chronic alcoholism," has died at the age of 91.

Young won two Emmys for his role in the '50s series *Father Knows Best*, as well as the hatred of millions of parents who could never measure up.

After *Father Knows Best*, young starred for ten years in *Marcus Welby M.D.*, winning an Emmy for his role, as well as the hatred of millions of doctors who could never measure up.

The succeeding years were no less prosperous for young's co-stars. "Bud" found his niche as an inventor and a motorcycle racer, while "Kitten" found a niche in her vein.

For over ten years, shows like *Father Knows Best* and *Ozzie and Harriet* represented "the" classic wholesome family sitcom, as well as a convenient launching pad for tragic drug addiction.

Young leaves behind four daughters and two grandchildren who will never measure up.

Jim Earl

Sports

Mourning Remembrance

Arnold Denker, 'Dean of American Chess'

Arnold Denker, famed U.S. chess champion, grandmaster and designated "Dean of American Chess," has died after a prolonged illness left him only able to hop in "L" shaped patterns, and gradually degenerated to the point where he could only walk straight ahead one step at a time, never backward or to the side, and with only the occasional diagonal movement.

A prolific writer on the subject of chess, Denker published such well-known titles as, *My Best Chess Moves, 1929 through 1976* and the lively follow-up, *My Worst Celibate Years, 1929 through 1976.*

It was just last June that the U.S. Chess Federation gave him the title "Dean of American Chess" for his achievements in the game, but mostly it was just a way of getting him off their backs.

Friends say until the very end, Denker took special pride in his collection of Chess memorabilia and could frequently be seen polishing his bishop.

Denker requested he be buried way back in the cupboard behind those old board games the kids never use anymore.

Jim Earl

Ben Hogan, Golf Legend

Ben Hogan, considered the greatest golfer in the history of sports, is dead after suffering a massive pulmonary embolism, or the kind of stroke from which no golfer could ever recover.

Hogan first discovered golf during puberty when he hit two good balls after stepping on a rake.

Even after enduring countless jokes like that, Hogan remained dedicated to the sport. And during the succeeding years he often spent the days "noodling" with his "little putter" in order to "cut a hard wood."

He finally won his first tournament in 1938. But the winnings were slim back in the Depression and all he received for his effort was a bowl of soup and a tumbleweed.

Hogan's life was not without hardship. During his later years, he suffered from elephantiasis and had to carry his bag around in a wheelbarrow.

During his illustrious career, Hogan won 63 tournaments, including nine major championships. But perhaps his greatest accomplishment was making golf the second most tedious sport to watch on TV after bowling.

For those of you not familiar with golf, the object of the game is to propel a small ball around a lawn using as little physical exertion as possible while making foreign policy decisions prolonging the Vietnam War.

Hogan requested his mashie niblet be preserved in a jar of formaldehyde right next to his father's mummified cleek.

Jim Earl

Annotation of Jim Earl's Mourning Remembrance
By his former stand-up comedy partner, Barry Lank

In some ways, this book is Jim Earl's own obituary - not because he's dead yet, nor because I'm going to kill him someday when the time is perfect. It's because these jokes tell you his entire life story, if you know what you're looking at. Jim does not throw jokes away. If he writes a gag that doesn't get picked up at one job, he will pitch it at each subsequent job for the rest of his life. So studying these articles is like brushing away the dust at a fossil dig, discovering earlier and earlier strata of Jim Earl's desperate and angry career, until we reach the primeval stage when he used oxen feces to write his first spec script for "F-Troop."

The following is a brief exegesis of this text, based on bad personal memories that cannot be erased until, as I said, the time is perfect. I sincerely hope my notes will help illuminate and ruin this book for you, as I am tired of Jim being funnier than I am.

As a general note, by the way: Jim has a special fondness for jokes that only he gets.

Sincerely,
Barry Lank, MA, MS, CELTA

*   *   *   *

p. 2, line 8

    Jim's use of hermaphrodites dates back to his college years, with his study of late medieval art. I believe he is saying here that his life would be a lot better is he just didn't need to get laid so badly.

p. 5

    Jim began quoting this piece of graffiti sometime in the late 1980s, and it crystallizes his fascination with taking massive dumps. This book will touch on all parts of this process - including the digestive tract itself, food contamination and the frustration that attends intestinal blockage. For Jim, taking a huge shit is a proud statement of some kind.

    Also, we drank a lot at Max's because it was down the street from the Holy City Zoo comedy club, where we performed stand-up pretty much every night of our lives from 1985 to 1993.

p. 25, paragraph 1

    Jokes about Carrot Top may seem overdone these days, but Jim is a pioneer in the field, having started making them before anyone quite knew who Carrot Top was. Jim, significantly, began making fun of comedy before he actually started doing comedy.

P. 31, paragraph 4

    Throughout this book, you will notice sections of technical language that apparently come straight from an encyclopedia or instruction manual. Partly, this is just a theme for this project. Party, it allows Jim to copy and paste whole sections for these articles without actually writing anything. But mostly, Jim has an obsession with dry language and jargon. For him, the funniest part of this whole book may well be the line "Repeat steps 9 through 12."

p. 35, paragraph 3
> Jim's mother was from Kansas, and Jim often used to visit there, watching the flat horizon and listening to his distant cousins talk about "the queers" and describe horrible farming accidents.

p. 36
> Jim has an interest in Nazis that is frankly astounding for a non-Jew.

p. 41, paragraph 2
> This is the book's first of many self-references to the joke-writing process itself. Jim and I were always one of the most meta acts on the San Francisco, circuit, leading some colleagues to call our work "anti-comedy." They didn't mean it in a nice way.

p. 47, paragraph 3
> This is the first time Jim tells the reader to be quiet. Later in the book, he will also tell you to get off his back, and, on three separate occasions, to shut up. He means it.

p. 53, paragraph 1
> This joke formula dates back to approximately the mid-1980s. When performing it, nightclub comedians would say the last part really loud - "hundred pounds" - while leaning so far into the microphone that it was considered acceptable just to put it in you mouth.

p. 73
> When Jim first became vegetarian in the early-to-mid 1980s (for a woman he was dating, by the way), he swore he'd never get self-righteous about it. Seriously. He said that. But the temptation became too much - partly because of Jim just enjoys self-righteousness a lot, partly because jokes about meat opened a natural channel for his fascination with bacteria and constipation.

p. 81, paragraphs 2 and 3
> I cannot fucking believe Jim put this in the book. Do you even know what the hell he's talking about here? Of course not - because you're not watching a show at the Laff Stop comedy club in Claremont, Calif., in the late 1970s. Jim worked there for a couple of years after high school, and that's where the club manager/house emcee/Jim's boss Adam Berenson regularly told the following joke:
>
>> "Welcome to ... Name That Object! Our guest panelists tonight are Prince Charles, Queen Elizabeth and the Duke of Windsor. And now, we'll tell the audience the object, before the panelists try to guess what it is."
>>
>> [IN MUTED, ANNOUNCER VOICE] "The object is ... a horse's dick. A horse's ... dick."
>>
>> [LOUD HOST VOICE AGAIN] "All right, Prince Charles, you ask the first question."
>>
>> [PRINCE CHARLES VOICE] "Is the object ... edible?"
>>
>> [HOST VOICE] "Uh ... judges? [BELL SOUND] Yes! The judges say the object is edible. Queen Elizabeth, your turn."
>>
>> [PAUSE]

Jim Earl

[SQUEAKY QUEEN ELIZABETH VOICE] "Is it a horse's dick?"

This was Jim's favorite joke in 1980.

P. 88

Did I mention Jim never throws jokes away? The ice cream flavors in this article come from a sketch called "Galaxy of Flavors," which he and I wrote in the late 1980s or early 1990s, at a Baskin-Robbins in San Francisco.

p. 105

Donuts are extremely important to Jim, and have always been among the extremely limited range of things he eats.

One night in the mid-1980s, Jim, our friends Will Chandler, Erik Tilgass and I were in Glendora at our favorite donut shop - now called The Donut Man (the best drive-through donuts anywhere, by the way). And we got into a long debate over whether donuts have souls. Fact: The argument actually turned serious, and almost ended in a fistfight.

p. 121, paragraph 8

Ah, the old "Getting turned on by something you couldn't possibly get turned on by" bit - the first of two times we'll see this. Jim likes this joke probably because he himself is turned on by just about everything.

p. 132, paragraph 2 ("... nibble on his jig wobbler ...")

There is a certain amount of Johnny Carson in Jim's writing.

p. 137, paragraph 3

In 1996, when Jim was developing a solo act, he did a bit in which he'd tell a joke, pause, then say "Ah, who am I kiddin' I got cancer."

p. 144, paragraph 4

The comic strip "Fred Bassett," of course, is like weak tea. It runs in newspapers internationally, yet has no discernible affect on readers. But I suspect Jim likes it because he had a basset hound when he was a kid (named Woodrow Wilson - I'm not kidding), and bassets are his favorite dogs.

p. 145, graph 3

Jim loves obscure, historical slang - as you will see when he wildly whacks off to it on page 181. I first noticed this habit in the early 1980s after Jim read some book about shipboard life in the 19th century, and walked around for at least a year afterwards mumbling in archaic mariners' jargon. He even quotes that book on Page 170, paragraph 5 ("... his sadistic cabin master..."), and partly summarizes the plot during the rant on page 238, graph 4 ("I Don't Care If You Are My Best Friend's Son Who Was Entrusted To Me For Training on the High Seas").

Jim's taste for this kind of argot has had a profound effect on this book, particularly during long parts of it when he didn't feel like writing actual jokes.

p. 205, paragraph 5

Ray Kroc, of course, made McDonald's a nationwide chain. I still remember when Jim constantly ate at McDonald's. In fact, he and either Will or Erik or both once went to something like seven McDonald's in one day, making sure to eat something at each one. I don't know exactly what happened on that trip, but Jim, Will and Erik all eventually turned vegetarian at some point years later, and Jim keeps writing about difficult bowel movements.

p. 206, paragraph 4

> Jim's parodies of observational comedy long predate the TV show "Seinfeld" and come out of the late 1980s, when one comedian after another started wearing sweaters onstage and making harmless observations about socks and road signs. All those comics are now old enough to need those sweaters around the house.

p. 217, paragraph 3

> Jim has been repeating the line "Moe, Larry, the cheese!" literally for as long as I've known him.

p. 228, paragraph 6

> In 1986 or so, Jim and I got jobs writing scripts for a pornographic phone line. I was meeting one day with the producers at their home (I forget if Jim was with me - he tended to avoid it) when the director came out of a recording studio where he'd been working with one of the voice actresses. And he said – and this is an exact quote – "Well ... she's crying."

p. 247, paragraph 2

> I am frankly surprised we got this far into the book before hitting a "save your urine in jars" reference - a pet obsession of Jim's that dates at least as far back as the 1985 publication of Michael Drosnin's "Citizen Hughes." Perhaps this delay means Jim is maturing! This is really a hopeful sign!

p. 253, paragraph 2

> Jim wrote the Q-tip joke when he worked at the Laff Stop in 1979, before he ever went on stage.

> * Author's Note: I have never met Barry Lank.

Jim Earl

Afterword

By Rachel Maddow

Jim Earl is a dark, dark, dark little ray of darkness, a man who can shame even the brightest sunshine into toning it down a little.

I alternated between reading this book out loud to my girlfriend, cracking up -- *her heart Gestapoed!* -- and shaking my head, muttering to myself that this is… just… *wrong*. Wrong wrong wrong. Occasionally deeply wrong.

But dammit, the unrelenting boosterism of everyone looking for the silver lining all the time requires the relief of someone pointing out the cloud there in the middle, the big stormy one killing people with the hail and the lightning bolts. That's Jim, the cloud guy. The guy whose book of fake obituaries has now made me unable to consider eating chicken again.

I have a T-shirt with Jim's name on it because at Air America Radio, we named our corporate softball team The Jim Earls. He was the only thing we could all agree on. Jim was so unrelentingly honest and uncompromising, it made sense to make a mascot of him -- the guy stands for something.

At one of our many going-out-of-business meetings with one of our many owners, there was raised the somewhat delicate matter of whether or not our health insurance premiums had been paid. Upon arriving at the fact that our employee "contributions" had not actually been contributed toward the insurance we all thought we had, in this hushed, polite meeting, suddenly there was Jim Earl. Standing, pointing, *j'accuse!*-style, yelling at the top of his lungs in a voice way deeper than you'd expect: "THIEVERY!".

It was hilarious. And he was right! And he wasn't joking. And Air America is no more, and Jim Earl still is. Accusing, wielding honesty like a cudgel. A terrifying, uncompromising dark, dark soul who is basically right. Right right right. Even when he makes you squirm. I believe in Jim Earl, I love this guy.

Jim Earl

About the Author

Jim Earl's life is none of your goddamned business. So shut up.

But if you must know: he used to write for *The Daily Show With Jon Stewart* and was awarded an Emmy and a Peabody Award for his sacrifice. But more important, he played the accountant in *Pootie Tang*, and got a free towel out of it.

He is also a man, who for over fifty years, lovingly wrote and performed his "Mourning Remembrance" segments for *Marc Maron's Morning Sedition* show on Air America Radio.

You can currently hear him perform on various podcasts including Marc Maron's *WTF* podcast and *The Jimmy Dore Show*.

His band, The Clutter Family, is about to release its 2nd CD, *Freak IT!*

Jim has three livers. And in his spare time, he likes to laugh at death and eat nectarines.

www.JimEarl.com
www.facebook.com/TheClutterFamily

Mourning Remembrance

Jim Earl

About the End of This Book

This is the end of this book. And shut up.

Made in the USA
Lexington, KY
03 April 2012